The Sea is all about us

by
Sarah Fraser Robbins
and
Clarice Yentsch

D0967517

QH
105
.M4
R62

A guidebook
to the marine
environments
of Cape Ann
and other northern
New England waters

LIBRARY
SOUTHERN MAINE VOCATIONAL
TECHNICAL INSTITUTE

The Sea Is All About Us

Sarah Fraser Robbins and Clarice M. Yentsch

Published by
The Peabody Museum of Salem
East India Square
Salem, MA 01970

"... the sea is all about us ..."
appears in T. S. Eliot's *The Dry Salvages*
from *Four Quartets*
Harcout Brace Jovanovich, Inc. publishers

QH   Robbins, Sarah Fraser.
105
.M4   The sea is all about us
R62

574.92145 R53

©copyright 1973 by Sarah Fraser Robbins and Clarice M. Yentsch
all rights reserved
Library of Congress catalog card number 73-79516
ISBN 87577-046-0
Printed in the United States of America
Text design by David Ford

Dedication

To Carlton and Chandler
and the new generation
in hopes that they will know,
understand and preserve the sea
that is all about us.

Preface

In the past, most of the residents and visitors of the Cape Ann area have been content to delight in the delicacy of seafood, shop in quaint shops, and breathe deeply the luxury of clean maritime air. The fascinating geology and biology of the area were often overlooked. The trend is reversing, however. Suddenly there is a renaissance of man's curiosity toward his environment, and a desire to appreciate and preserve it.

This guidebook is intended for those who wish to familiarize themselves with the seashore populations and the general ecology around Cape Ann and other northern New England waters. It is in part a compilation of information available in some twenty to thirty other books. Many more species occur in the local waters than are covered here. Representative species most commonly encountered have been selected.

Illustrations were done by Mary Ann Lash, University of Massachusetts Marine Station, with the exception of some occurring on pages 25, 27, 28, 29, 30, 31, 32, 35, 36, 37, 39 and 41, which were the work of Isabel Natti, University of Massachusetts Marine Station. Fish illustrations on pages 130 through 143 are from FISHES OF THE GULF OF MAINE by Henry Bigelow and William C. Schroeder, by permission of William C. Schroeder, Museum of Comparative Zoology, Harvard University, Cambridge.

Photographs were the work of Mark Sexton, Photographer at the Peabody Museum, Salem, with the exception of pages 7 and 147 by Peter Tuttle; page 23 by C. Lewis; pages 47 and 125 by Barry Spacklin; pages 49 and 50 by Dr. Ken Read, Tom Stack & Associates; pages 57, 62, 65, 92 by Patricia Morse; pages 68, 143, and 144 by Peter Prybot; and page 90 by Col. Eugene S. Clark, Jr. Photographs on pages 10, 15, 17, 19, 22, 76, and 145 were by Laureen Naismith, University of Massachusetts Marine Station. Photographs on pages 46, 48, 53, 54, 55, 58, 61, 63, 66, 67, 77, 91, 92, 94, 100, 104, 106, 109, 121, 125, 127 and 146 were by the senior author.

Our special thanks to each of the above and to the following:
For guidance —
Edward S. Gilfillan, III, University of Massachusetts Marine Station
Sally Ingalls, Curator of Natural History, Peabody Museum of Salem
Patricia Morse, Edwards Marine Laboratory, Nahant
James Sears, Hampshire College, Amherst
Charles S. Yentsch, University of Massachusetts Marine Station
For perseverance —
Jean Baxter
Dorothy Addams Brown
Arlene N. Conner
Elmer and Caroline Foye
For inspiration and encouragement —
John Kieran
For patience —
David Ford
Russell Williamson
For assistance with portions of the text material —
Stephanie Bradley, University of Massachusetts Marine Station
Ralph Dexter, Kent State University, Kent, Ohio
Ian Morris, University College of London, W.C.1, England
Peter Prybot, University of Massachusetts Marine Station
Edgar Webber, Keuka College, Keuka, New York
For assistance with specimens —
Barry Spacklin, Edwards Marine Laboratory, Northeastern University
John Valois, Marine Biological Laboratory, Woods Hole
For assistance with the manuscript —
Bridget Bryson, Beverly
Nicole Daley, University of Massachusetts Marine Station
Tina Ketchopulos, University of Massachusetts Marine Station
Martina Matthiessen, University of Massachusetts Marine Station
Lois Strube, University of Massachusetts Marine Station
For cooperation
Cape Ann Society for Marine Science, Inc., Gloucester
Edwards Marine Laboratory of Northeastern University, Nahant
Massachusetts Audubon Society Lincoln
New England Aquarium, Boston
Peabody Museum of Salem
University of Massachusetts Marine Station, Gloucester

Our sincere thanks to each of these persons and institutions for their competent help and encouragement — and our thanks to the countless enthusiastic students of all ages who have confirmed over and over again that there is a need for a project such as this.

Sarah Fraser Robbins
Clarice M. Yentsch
Gloucester
May 1973

Table of Contents

Environmental Factors Affecting Marine Organisms

SALINITY

A first dip in the ocean, and the most obvious and distinctive characteristic of sea water is observed by even the youngest of children. The water doesn't taste good; it burns the eyes; it is easier to float in it . . . in short, the water is salty.

Sea water contains about 3.5 percent salt. When evaporation is greater than precipitation, the salinity is greater. When precipitation is greater than evaporation, the salinity is less. Ocean scientists write salinity in terms of parts per thousand; therefore, 3.5 percent would be 35 parts per thousand (35 o/oo).

The salinity around Cape Ann normally ranges from 22 to 33 o/oo. Greater variation is possible in small coves and tide pools. The salinity of a tide pool can range much greater than this in one day's time. Some organisms are exceedingly resistant to salinity changes.

Sea water tastes little different than common table salt (NaCl) dissolved in water, yet it is more complex. Sea salt contains every natural element — that is, over 100 different chemical elements.

Four elements make up 95 percent of all the salts in sea water. The common four chemicals in sea water and the percentages in which they are present are:

Chlorine	(Cl^-)	55%
Sodium	(Na^+)	30%
Sulfate	$(SO_4^=)$	7% (composed of sulfur and oxygen)
Magnesium	(Mg^{++})	3%
		95% of total salts by weight

Minor constituents are found in extremely small amounts in the oceans, yet many trace elements are essential for growth. Some animals and plants tend to concentrate various trace elements. For example, large algae (kelp)

1

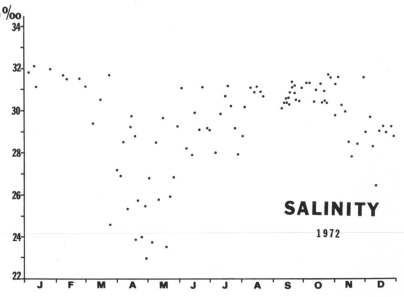

Salinity data at Hodgkin's Cove, Gloucester, 1972, in parts per thousand.

concentrate iodine, and are even harvested for iodine. Examples of other trace elements include iron (Fe), tin (Sn), titanium (Ti), cobalt (Co), cadmium (Cd), and chromium (Cr).

DISSOLVED GASES

The source of gases dissolved in sea water is through photosynthesis and the atmosphere. If one measures these gases, one finds them present in different quantities in the ocean, as compared with the atmosphere.

	Atmosphere	Ocean
Nitrogen (N_2)	78%	10%
Oxygen (O_2)	21%	10%
Carbon dioxide (CO_2)	0.04%	30%

Note that the carbon dioxide in the ocean is about 750 times the concentration of carbon dioxide in the atmosphere. The large difference is due to the life processes in the sea water, as well as the great solubility of carbon dioxide in water. Plants undergo photosynthesis in the light with the net effect of giving off oxygen to the water.

$$CO_2 + H_2O \xrightarrow{\text{chlorophyll \& light}} CH_2O + O_2 \text{ (photo-synthesis)}$$

In effect, the opposite occurs with respiration.

$$CH_2O + O_2 \longrightarrow H_2O + CO_2 \text{ (respiration)}$$

The animals undergo respiration with the net effect of giving off carbon dioxide to the water, both day and night. Plants undergo respiration, therefore giving off carbon dioxide. However, during daylight, much more oxygen, resulting from photosynthesis, is produced than carbon dioxide consumed. Daily measurements of the fluctuations of carbon dioxide and oxygen content of sea water reveal the amount of biological activity present.

Below the photic zone, zone of photosynthesis, there is relatively little oxygen. Conditions of no oxygen (anaerobic conditions), though not uncommon in fresh water, are rare in the oceans. Areas such as fjords, where the bottom features cut off circulation, are examples of anaerobic waters in the oceans. The only known anaerobic areas around Cape Ann are below the surface of mudflats and at the bottom of the harbors of Gloucester and Rockport, where the dumping of sewage has put an unusual demand on the supplies of available oxygen.

Nitrogen in the form of atmospheric or gaseous nitrogen (N_2) can be used by very few plants. Most phytoplankton use nitrogen in the forms of nitrate, nitrite and ammonia. The few specialized organisms using gaseous nitrogen are called nitrogen-fixers. On land, these are primarily small microscopic bacteria found on roots of legume plants such as peas and alfalfa. In the ocean, the nitrogen-fixers are microscopic bacteria and blue-green algae. *Calothrix*, the blue-green alga at the high-tide line, is known to fix nitrogen.

LIGHT

Photosynthesis requires light. In most parts of the world's oceans, light capable of causing photosynthesis penetrates the top 100 meters (300 feet) of water. The layer which light does penetrate is called the photic zone, euphotic zone, or the zone of light. Plants of the oceans obviously must live in this zone. Therefore, most of the animal life of the ocean is also in this zone, or migrates to this zone in search of food. This is a thin skin when compared to the vast ocean depths of over 10,500 meters, (6½ miles).

Light can be: 1) absorbed; 2) reflected; 3) scattered by particles in water or by the water itself. Sunlight is composed of all wave lengths of light; one part is invisible ultraviolet (responsible for tans and sunburns); a second part, the various colors of visible light, which, when combined, appear white to the eye; and a third part is the invisible infrared (responsible for about one-half of the sun's heat).

In water, the ultraviolet and the infrared are absorbed rapidly. At the depth of one meter, the remaining light is restricted to visible light. At 5 meters, a person underwater can barely see any red color — meaning that all the red light has been absorbed. Red objects appear gray or black. Skin divers are familiar with this phenomenon. For underwater photographs, red filters are used. The filter holds back blue and green light, and lets the small amount of red light pass through to the film.

Color is important to marine life. Ocean plants grow where they get appropriate light, and animals occur where they are least conspicuous. There is a trend for green algae to grow nearest the surface. The brown algae occur below the green algae, and red algae are frequently found toward the bottom of the photic zone. Many fish have blue upper portions, inconspicuous when looking down at them, and silver under portions, inconspicuous when looking up at them. Deep water organisms are often red, therefore being inconspicuous as they appear black to the observer.

PLANT GROWTH SUBSTANCES

The so-called limiting elements are essential to the growth of plants in the oceans. These chemicals, in forms of the elements nitrogen (N) and phosphorus (P), limit plant growth. As you may recognize, these are the common chemicals in fertilizers for lawns and gardens. Every good garden needs these — including the garden of the sea. If there is lush plant life, many animals will also be found, as the animals are dependent on the plant life as a source of food. The compounds of nitrogen are nitrate (NO_3), nitrite (NO_2), and ammonia (NH_3); and the compound of phosphorus is phosphate (PO_4).

Prior to abundant blooms of plants in the sea, these chemicals are high in concentration. The plants then utilize these chemicals by incorporating them into proteins and other cellular materials, and the concentrations of these chemicals is reduced thereby. Ocean biologists refer to the drifting plant population as phytoplankton.

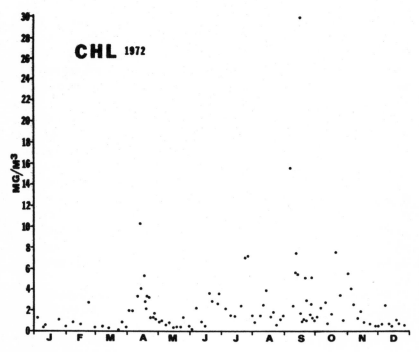

Phytoplankton concentration at Hodgkin's Cove, Gloucester, 1972,
in terms of milligrams per cubic meter of chlorophyll.
The high peak in September is due to the red tide outbreak.

FOOD FOR ANIMAL GROWTH

Phytoplankton is important as it is the major food source of the sea. The
plants are eaten by the animals, and the animal population increases until the
food runs out. Eventually, the limiting nutrients are used up, and the plant
population begins to decrease, and subsequently the animal population
decreases. Decay resulting from death and fecal waste contribute largely
to the P and N pool in the oceans. In the temperate and tropical regions,
where there is a temperature barrier (thermocline), P and N often occur
as particulate matter and sink below this barrier, and are consequently
separated from the potentially productive zones. Once these chemicals are
circulated and are again in the photic zone, the cycle continues and more
phytoplankton are produced, providing more food for more zooplankton.

TEMPERATURE

Several books have been written on the uniqueness of pure water, H_2O. Ice — frozen water — floats. Water has a freezing point of $0°C$ ($32°F$). Water boils at $100°C$ ($212°F$). It needs more heat to cause it to evaporate than any other substance (called latent heat of evaporation), and holds or retains heat very well; therefore, its nickname is the thermo-regulator.

The temperatures found in ocean waters range from $-2°C$ to $+30°C$ ($28°F$ to $86°F$). How can one have water and not ice at $-2°C$? As soon as salts are added to water, the properties of the freezing point and boiling point are altered. The freezing point is lowered and the boiling point is raised, depending upon how salty the water is. Sea water generally needs to be below $-2°C$ in order to freeze. Sea ice, such as forms in coves, is not very salty at all. When sea water freezes, the ice crystals formed are nearly fresh water, and the salt goes into the rest of the water, thus making the remaining water super salty. Freezing and thawing sea water is one method of removing salt (desalination), which can result in drinkable water from ocean water.

Sea smoke is a fog that is formed when the dew point (the temperature

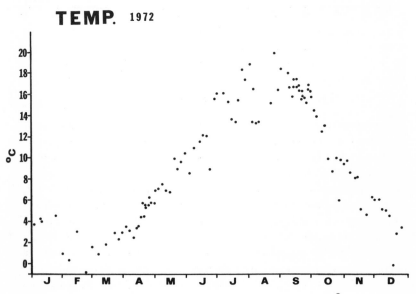

TEMP. 1972

Temperature data at Hodgkin's Cove, Gloucester, 1972, in $°C$.

Sea ice

at which a vapor begins to condense) is reached at low temperatures. This indicates that the water temperature is in excess of the air temperature. This weird, fascinating occurrence is most frequent at temperatures near $-17°C$ ($0°F$).

OCEAN CURRENTS

Ocean waters are in motion. The water around Cape Ann today may be near Cape Cod tomorrow. The first mapping of ocean currents was done by Benjamin Franklin. He noted that it took mail ships longer to go from England to the United States than it did for them to go from the United States to England. The current he mapped was the Gulf Stream — a wind-driven current.

The Gulf Stream off the eastern coast of the United States in the Atlantic Ocean is one of the strongest currents known to man. It is like a river within the ocean. The volume of water flowing is 70 times greater than all the land rivers combined. The path of the Gulf Stream water passes North America, flowing toward Europe. The winds that drive the flow are the Trade Winds in the lower latitudes and the Westerlies in the higher latitudes.

Note that in the other oceans of the Northern Hemisphere the pattern of winds and wind-driven currents is similar, and the pattern in the Southern Hemisphere is reversed. Upwelling nearshore vertical currents bring colder nutrient-rich water from great depths into the photic zone. A barrier to vertical movement often occurs between waters of different temperatures. This is called the thermocline. In the middle latitudes, e.g., Cape Ann, when the surface water is warmed, a thermocline develops and is present in spring, summer and fall. Winter cools the surface, and the thermocline is disrupted by vertical currents.

TIDES

The organisms covered in this guidebook are subjects of the tides. Tides cause massive water movement. They result because of gravitational attraction. All bodies attract one another. The earth and moon attract each other. The earth and sun attract each other. The moon and the sun are the two largest, most effective bodies to influence tides. The land surfaces of the earth are pulled to the moon and sun as much as the ocean surfaces; however, the land surface is not flexible, while the surface of the ocean is. We all know that the sun is much larger than the moon, yet its effect on

Generalized pattern of ocean currents

tides is much less than the effect of the moon. The reason for this is that the sun is so much farther away from the earth than the moon is. Force differs as distance. The sun has only one-half the pulling power of the moon.

A bulge or lump of water rotates around the earth beneath the moon. As the earth rotates and the bulge hits land, water piles up and high tides are produced. The time of the tides changes daily. It takes the earth one day and fifty minutes to reach the place the moon has reached in one day. Thus, the high tide comes approximately one hour later each day. The sun and moon alignment dictates the extent of the high or low tide. These include spring tide (full and new moon) and neap tide (moon's effect at right angles to the sun — therefore, one-half moon). With each tide, there is a flow — called the flood on the incoming tide, and the ebb on the out-going tide.

Local conditions have a tremendous effect on the height of the tides. Consequently, they are predicted only locally. Tide tables are based on past observations. On Cape Ann, we follow a Boston tide table with minor altera-tions. The alterations are as follows: Annisquam 0.0 minutes (8.5 tidal range); Gloucester −5 (8.7); Ipswich +5 (8.7); Nahant 0.0 (9.0); Newburyport +50 (7.8); Rockport −5 (8.6); Salem −5 (9.0).

Freak examples of tides occur at some locations such as the Bay of Fundy, Nova Scotia, which is the edge of a basin. There, tides often exceed

Low tide, Folly Cove, Rockport

High tide, Folly Cove, Rockport

50 feet! The island of Nantucket off Cape Cod in Massachusetts is the other extreme. It is located at the center of a basin, and the high tide cancels the low tide. We are all familiar with this as the slosh at the edge and calm in the center of a bathtub. At Nantucket tides are very slight, often only 3.0 feet. The island of Tahiti in the Pacific Ocean is also the center of a basin. It is near the equator. It has no moon effect, but does have a solar or sun effect. Every day there is a high tide at 12 noon and 12 midnight, and a low tide at 6 a.m. and 6 p.m. In most cases, as on Cape Ann, tides are semi-diurnal, meaning that there are two high tides and two low tides daily.

SUBSTRATE

Wherever sea and land meet, there is a potential substrate for attached marine organisms, called benthos. Mountain systems, valleys and canyons exist beneath the sea surface. There are mountains that exceed the height of Mt. Everest, the highest mountain on the surface of the land, and canyons greater in depth than the Grand Canyon, the most extensive canyon on the surface of the land. Nearly three-fourths of the earth's surface is covered by water. The land masses are broad. At the ocean's edge, the land gradually tapers off — referred to as the continental shelf. Eventually, the land drops off rather steeply — the continental slope. The continental shelf is a great place for most offshore fishing. Offshore drilling for oil and offshore dredging for sand and gravel also take place on the continental shelf.

The average depth of the oceans is 3800 meters (about 2 miles). The deepest known part is over 10,500 meters deep (about 6½ miles). At great depths along the ocean bottom the temperature and salinity change very little. Organisms are scarce. This is in great contrast to the shallow bottom and the intertidal area which is richly inhabited by a variety of plants and animals. The shallow seashore is without doubt the most widely studied part of the sea. This is primarily because of its easy access and its ability to arouse the curiosity of the shorebound scientist and layman.

It is interesting to note that the energy fixed by the seashore plants is estimated to be only between 1 to 10 percent of the energy fixed by the phytoplankton of the open ocean. However, seashore life is of considerable interest as far as endurance of plants and animals to extreme changes in salinity, temperature, nutrients and light. Many organisms find suitable substrate in the intertidal area.

Marine Environments

CAPE ANN

Cape Ann is an island moated by a tidal seaway — a part of and lying off Essex County, Massachusetts — about thirty miles north of Boston. It is rocky with hard granite bedrock on the seaward side jutting boldly out into the Gulf of Maine, and separates Ipswich Bay from Massachusetts Bay. There are a few sandy beaches around the shoreline, and salt marshes to the west, where the Annisquam River, a seaway, severs the Cape from the mainland. This man-made cut through the southern end of the salt marshes into Gloucester Harbor made Cape Ann an island which is joined to the mainland by the Blynman drawbridge at Gloucester Harbor and by the A. Piatt Andrew bridge on Route 128.

During the periods of Continental glaciation, Cape Ann was covered with ice and was alternately covered and uncovered in the interglacial and melting periods. Dogtown Common, a deserted settlement from which the dogs were last to leave, is a terminal moraine in the middle of the Cape. All along the shore in the Bass Rocks, Eastern Point, Rockport, Pigeon Cove, Lanesville and Annisquam areas there are evidences of glaciation: erratic and perched boulders, glacial scratches and bedrock scraped smooth by the ice.

The rocky shores of Cape Ann are of two types, both interesting for their intertidal plants and animals. One type is the sea-cut cliff, examples of which can be found at Bass Rocks, Lanesville, Bay View, Pigeon Cove, and Halibut Point, where the bedrock extends below the sea surface and there are many tide pools. The other type of shore is the boulder beach, where rounded, wave-worn boulders vary in size from rocks one to two meters in diameter, as on the back shore of Bass Rocks, to smaller stones of the shingle and pebble beaches such as Long Beach and Pebbly Beach. These gradually sloping shores are in contrast to the bedrock areas, which usually fall off abruptly.

13

THE ROCKY SHORE

Plant and animal life on the rocky shore can be separated into six general zones, beginning with the Black Zone, which marks the average high point that the sea reaches upon the land. The Black Zone is covered by microscopic blue-green algae, which are so dense that they make a black line of varying widths along the rocks. These blue-green algae exist at high-tide level all around the world wherever the sea meets the land on rocks.

Just below the Black Zone lie the Periwinkle Zone and Barnacle Zone, named after the dominant animals. There is no definite territorial line for these animals, and indeed the zones often intermingle with each other. Barnacles and periwinkles can be found penetrating the Rockweed Zone (the next zone seaward) and sometimes into the edge of the Irish Moss Zone. Both periwinkles and barnacles are equipped to withstand desiccation (drying out), and can live very successfully in an area that is dry up to 70 percent of the time.

The Rockweed Zone lies in the middle intertidal area, and is characterized by the brown seaweeds that live there, such as the sea wrack, *Fucus,* and the knotted wrack, *Ascophyllum,* which are long, brown seaweeds with conspicuous float bladders that are firmly attached to most of the rocks. They hang limply when the tide is out and float upwards as the tide rises until they are completely erect at high tide. They sway back and forth, dampening the effect of wave action, and providing a sheltered environment for many intertidal plants and animals.

The Irish Moss Zone is down lower from the high-tide line and is exposed only during the very low tides which occur twice a month. The short, dark red tufts of Irish moss, *Chondrus crispus,* cover the lower rocks like a carpet, in sharp contrast with the brown Rockweed Zone, the white Barnacle Zone, the Periwinkle Zone and the Black Zone above.

The Laminarian or Kelp Zone is exposed only at the very lowest tides, which occur four times a year. This zone extends down as far as light usable for photo-synthesis can penetrate — about 30 meters in Folly Cove, and 200 meters in very clear tropical water. Light penetration varies from place to place depending upon clarity of the water. The Kelp Zone is the dwelling place of many animals that can survive only continually submerged in water; sponges, hydroids, anemones, certain mollusks, echinoderms, arthropods, tunicates, and fish. Many of these animals may be found higher in the intertidal zones, but only in tide pools that never dry up.

Tide pools occur in all the zones. The upper pools, in the splash area or Periwinkle Zone are sporadically replenished with sea water, and consequently

Rocky shore

are subject to variations caused by land temperatures. They may freeze long before the ocean does. They evaporate in hot sun and strong winds, and thereby concentrate their salinity, that is, become saltier than the sea. At times during August, they are reduced to a crust of salt crystals. After heavy rains and floods they become much less salty. Some tide pools in the middle zones will contain animals and plants characteristic of a deeper zone because the conditions present are similar to those in the zones below. Tide pools in the Irish Moss Zone often contain kelp and associated animals. Tide pools are always a good place to explore.

The edge of the tide is a fragile environment which in its delicate natural balance can easily be destroyed by interference. The building of piers, jetties and sewage outfalls, and the dumping of trash or industrial wastes into the ocean can be devastating. Overcollecting can be destructive. In the intertidal areas, look and touch only. Examine plants and animals carefully. Overturn stones to see what is clinging to them or living underneath, but always turn that stone back. To leave it overturned alters the environment completely and needlessly kills many organisms. Take photographs or make careful drawings for your notebook, but collect only dead material. Use unbreakable plastic containers from which to observe the organisms and then return them to a tide pool.

SANDY AND MUDDY BEACHES

Whenever there are waves along the shore, we find sand and mud in suspension. Water currents carry these sand and mud particles all around Cape Ann to the marshes and into the estuaries. Wherever the flow of water is slowed, the sediment will settle. The heavy material drops out first and then finer and finer sediments are deposited. An apron of mud is formed along the marsh. Coarse or fine sand is deposited in the creek beds. Quite pebbly beaches are formed in the coves of the rocky shores. After a big storm, fine sand is everywhere — from up in the splash area to between pebbles and stones on

Sandy-muddy beach

rocky beaches. Wherever sand is found, we find sand dwellers, and often they inhabit both rocky shore and sandy shore in places where sand collects between or under boulders. Rocky shore animals are found where rocks occur on beaches or marshes. In general, the sandy shore dwellers are more common in Ipswich Bay which has a hard sand bottom, while the mud dwellers are prevalent in Gloucester Harbor and the marshlands.

SALT MARSHES

There are extensive salt marshes (about 900 acres) on and around Cape Ann. Most are found on the West Gloucester or inland side, bordering the Annisquam, Essex and Little Rivers, and in back of Wingaersheek Beach. The Good Harbor marshes once extended to Eastern Avenue, but construction of a shopping center changed that area drastically. These marshes are legacies of the great Continental ice sheet that melted only 9000 years ago.

As the ice melted and the runoff water returned to the sea, two things happened. The land, relieved of the great weight of ice, rose, as did the water level of the ocean. Many freshwater swamps were drowned by salt water. Many valleys were also partially drowned and cut off from the open sea by sand spits formed by the longshore currents that flow down our coast. These shallow protected areas soon filled up with silt and mud. Seeds of marsh grass were carried in on the feet of migrating shore birds. These seeds grew and the marshes began. As the change in levels of land and sea continued, the marshes grew until at one time there were hundreds of kilometers of uncontaminated saltwater marshes bordering the Atlantic coast from the St. Lawrence River to Florida. The changes in water level affected the entire coast, not just that part covered by the glacier.

For years, the coastal marshes were an integral part of saltwater farms, protecting the upland meadows from winter northeasters and serving as summer pasturage and winter fodder for the cattle in the form of salt hay. As the country became industrialized, and people began to move from farms to the city, the land was sold. Homes were built on the uplands. All too often marshes were filled in, dredged or used as dumps or for marinas. Now only one-third of the original Atlantic coast marshland is left.

Most people fail to realize that salt marshes and estuaries, where salt and fresh water meet, are the world's greatest nurseries of fish, shellfish, and water fowl as well as being buffer areas in the case of violent storms. Clams, oysters, crabs and mussels live in marshes, as do many kinds of food fish. Some, like shad, alewives, and striped bass, come through the marshes to spawn in fresh water and return at once to the sea. Others, like certain flounders (important food fish) spend part of the year feeding and growing in the marshes. Two-thirds of the commercial catch of fish and shellfish of the east coast of the United States spend part of their life cycle in marshes. The productivity per acre of a salt marsh is the highest of any place on earth.

The salt marsh community is very specialized. There is much adversity with which to contend: 1) changes in salinity of the water; 2) seasonal temperature changes of as much as 50° C (120° F); and 3) the fluctuations of the tide. A

Salt marsh

salt marsh is dominated by plants, especially the conspicuous grasses known as *Spartina*, or cord grass.

Seaward, just above the mid-tide level, occurs the stiff, broad-leaved grass which grows in spikes that can easily cut bare feet. It is also a cord grass, *Spartina alterniflora*. This plant bears white flowers in August. Like all grasses, *Spartina* is fertilized by pollen carried by the wind. The soft breezes of August blowing over the marsh, like wind on a green sea, are spreading the pollen, and the grass seed is being set for the coming year.

Spartina alterniflora is so well adapted to living in salt water most of the time (other plants die when their roots stand in salt water) that it must be immersed in salt water every day. The high-water cord grass, *S. patens*, is only inundated with salt water at the very high tides. Each of these plants is an indicator of how high the tide comes up and one may see the winding course of the little saltwater creeks in the marsh by following the line of dark green *S. alterniflora*, which grows along the mid-tide level and gives way to the lighter green expanse of *S. patens* on higher ground.

A saltwater marsh is made up of wet mud and underlying peat which has been building up for a long time. When the glacier melted and the first *Spartina alterniflora* was seeded and grew, mud and silt carried down by rivers and streams got caught in the roots and stems of the grass. The land was slowly built up and there came a time when the grass was well above mid-tide level so that *Spartina alterniflora* was replaced by *Spartina patens*. *S. alterniflora* continued to spread toward the ocean, and the marsh increased in size out to sea and up the upland meadows. As the marsh grew, certain plants and animals came to live in the marsh community. Many animals came into the marsh with the tide or came from the upland out onto the marsh at low tide. The actual marshland usually ends abruptly in a thatch bank that is vertically exposed on the sides of tidal creeks. Below this, there is a gently sloping apron of mud that ends in a sand or mud bank (occasionally a bed of clay) at the bottom of the creeks, and then a sand bar where the creeks enter the sea.

Organisms of the Marine Environment

PLANTS
Algae

Algae are simple and primitive plants as compared to the higher plants with which we are more familiar. Yet, there are tendencies toward specialization of cells and tissues. Some have complex structure and form, but none have true roots, stems or leaves. Algae absorb the carbon dioxide, water and nutrients needed through all their surfaces. Hence, roots, stems and leaves are not needed. Many algae species are single cells and some species are colonial. Others grow in filaments, branched filaments or sheet-like layers. Large complex algae have a root-like structure modified for attachment called a holdfast, a stem-like portion called a stipe, and a leaf-like structure called a blade. Algae with midribs can look exceedingly leaf-like.

Collecting and pressing algae is easily done with semi-absorbent paper such as sketch paper or herbarium paper and a container larger than the paper size. Lay the paper in the container and fill with sea water. Float and arrange a small amount of the alga over the paper. Lift the paper up gently and place between paper towel and newspaper under heavy books, or use a plant press. Dry overnight. There is generally sufficient adhesive on the surface of the alga for it to adhere to the paper; however, additional glue may be required for coarse algae such as *Ascophyllum* and *Fucus*. It is wise to label genus, species (both underlined; genus is capitalized, species is not), common name, collector's name, date and place of collection.

In general, algae are grouped and identified by color. Color is caused by a combination of photosynthetic pigments. Chlorophyll *a* is found in all green plants. There are numerous phyla of algae whose members are microscopic; only the macroscopic will be considered here. The major phyla of the macroscopic algae in the marine environment are the blue-green (Cyanophyta), the green (Chlorophyta), brown (Phaeophyta), and red (Rhodophyta). Characteristics of cell structure, cell wall, pigmentation, reproduction, growth patterns, motility, habitat, uses, and marine examples are given for each of these phyla, and the phylum Pyrophyta.

Blue-green algae — phylum Cyanophyta

The blue-greens are most simple in appearance. The cells lack a nucleus bound by a membrane. They also lack an organized chloroplast, having their chlorophyll scattered in pockets of the plasma membrane. The cell wall is composed of an outer gelatinous sheath. The blue-greens contain chlorophyll *a*, as do all photosynthetic plants (excluding bacteria). Their various colors (red, blue-green, black, pink) are due to a host of accessory pigments, most notably β-carotene, myxoxanthophyll, myxoxanthin, phycocyanin and phycoerythrin. The latter two pigments also occur in red algae. Asexual reproduction is accomplished by simple fission where the cell splits. The blue-greens can be unicellular, colonial, or as in most cases, filamentous. The individual cells tend to produce a sticky mucilage that holds newly divided cells together. Blue-greens lack flagellae or cilia. They move at the mercy of currents or winds or other outside physical forces. Some are attached. Blue-greens are greatly diversified and can live just about anyplace imaginable. They live in the sea, soil, fresh water, in the air, even in hot thermal springs. The blue-greens are extremely important to paleontologists interested in the very earliest days of life. Many ancient blue-greens are not too different from those living today.

Marine blue-greens are in our area. *Calothrix* produces a dark band on rocks in the upper tidal area. There are several species of *Calothrix* that are characteristic of the littoral zone. They are distinguished from one another by the

Calothrix sp.

aid of the microscope. Although microscopic individually, they form large obvious mats that are collectively known as the Black Zone at the top of the intertidal area. They occur around the world in this high-tide location. Like many blue-greens, they are somewhat capable of dissolving limestone and marble. This is suspected to be the result of secretions of oxalic acid. This action promotes erosion. *Calothrix* sp. is the most primitive alga found on Cape Ann. The cells of *Calothrix* sp. are arranged in a filament and are covered with a layer of jelly material known as the sheath. This layer prevents the cells from drying out when the tide is out. If the sheath itself dries, it forms a protective shell-like layer over the plants themselves. There is evidence that this organism is capable of fixing atmospheric nitrogen.

Fire algae – phylum Pyrophyta

The fire algae include the dinoflagellates. They are exclusively unicellular and flagellated. Many species have an obvious cell wall composed of plates. Although microscopic, at times they occur in sufficient quantities to discolor water. This phenomenon is referred to as red tide and red water. The dinoflagellates are sometimes classified as plants and sometimes as animals, because they possess characteristics of both. Some are bioluminescent, meaning that they are capable of giving off light by combining two chemicals produced within the cell. The dinoflagellates possess chlorophyll *a* and chlorophyll *c* as well as fucoxanthin pigments. Asexual reproduction is common and is accomplished by simple fission where the cells split. Sexual reproduction results from gamete production and fusion. Following sexual reproduction, or during adverse conditions, many dinoflagellates form cysts which are quite resistant to environmental stresses. There is evidence that shellfish ingesting either motile cells or cysts can become toxic. When the toxic shellfish are consumed by humans, the toxin affects the nervous system and the food poisoning known as Paralytic Shellfish Poisoning may result.

There is disturbing evidence that red tide appears to be increasing in

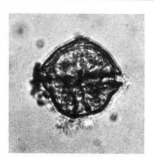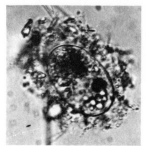

New England red tide organism: *Gonyaulax*
Left: motile cell from the water column, common during the spring, summer and autumn.
Right: resting cyst from sediments, common during the winter.

frequency and spreading in distribution. Due to the economic impact on the shellfishing industry and the public health threat, intensive research is under-way in an attempt to understand this organism and its toxins. Recent evidence indicates that the problem is indeed an oceanographic phenomenon, with vast subsurface maxima of the dinoflagellates occurring offshore during much of the summer. During certain meteorological conditions, the organisms are transported into the near-shore waters and thus interact with shellfish beds.

Green algae — phylum Chlorophyta

The green algae are far more differentiated than the blue-greens. Plastids of various numbers and shapes contain pigments. In some cases, plastids appear to respond to light by moving. The chloroplasts contain pyrenoids which are protein bodies used to store starch. The cells are governed by a distinct nucleus. The cell wall is composed primarily of cellulose and pectin. The green algae have pigments identical to higher plants. These include chlorophylls *a* and *b* plus carotenoids. The greens reproduce vegetatively, asexually by releasing zoospores, and sexually. Alternation of generation is quite prominent. Growth forms include unicellular, colonies, filaments, and flat sheets. Most green algae have motile stages at some time during their life cycles. Some unicells are motile most of their lives. Motility is accomplished by a stroking motion of flagellae. Greens occur in the sea, fresh water, or in the air. Only about 10% are marine, and they are quite specific as to where they will live. Many types of fresh water and marine greens act as indicators of pollution. This more or less is saying they appear when it is too late.

Enteromorpha sp. is commonly known as sea grass or maiden hair. There are a great many species of this genera and the classification is often confusing not only to the novice, but also to the specialist. In general, long thin green plants arise from a small disc at the base where it is attached to the rock or other substratum. It appears ribbon-like. Size can range from a few up to 50 centimeters in length. *Enteromorpha* sp. and another genus of similar form, *Monostroma* sp. are the most common algal inhabitants of tide pools. A feature most advantageous for this organism is its wide salinity tolerance. This can be noticed by the fact that it grows on hulls of boats traveling from fresh to salt water daily! Different species are found along the entire Atlantic coast.

Monostroma sp. greatly resembles *Ulva*, except that it is much more delicate. The delicacy results from the blade being only one cell layer thick in contrast to the multicellular blade of *Ulva*. *Monostroma* sp. is often found in tide pools. It grows up to 10 centimeters in diameter. When young, the plant looks like a sac; later the sac opens up to produce a flat to undulated light green blade. It is found all along northern New England shores.

   Ulva lactuca, commonly called **sea lettuce** (*lactuca* is the Latin word for lettuce) forms small to large flat sheets, occasionally with holes in its blade. It is very common, but not restricted to rocky shores near low water and below. It also occurs in quiet bays and salt marsh mud flats where it can be so dense as to completely cover the underlying mud . It is made into soup in the Orient and into salads in Scotland. *Ulva* has an inconspicuous holdfast from which the blade emerges immediately. There is no stipe. The plants occurring around Cape Ann are usually under 30 centimeters in diameter. In other areas of the world, however, species of *Ulva* can grow up to 1 meter in diameter. *Ulva* is found in somewhat protected areas. It is found growing on wood, rocks and coarse algae from Florida to Newfoundland.

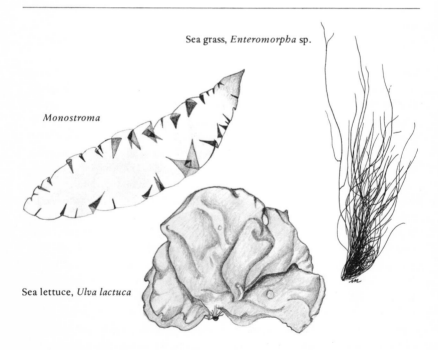

Sea grass, *Enteromorpha* sp.

Monostroma

Sea lettuce, *Ulva lactuca*

   Chaetomorpha sp. grows as a mass of wiry filaments from a holdfast at its base. It is commonly found as a tuft of tangled filaments floating or washed up on the shore. The masses are usually small, but can reach up to 20 centimeters. The yellowish or bright green filaments can be straight or curly, depending upon species. *Chaetomorpha atrovirens* is curly; *Chaetomorpha melagonium* is straight. Both are uncommon south of Cape Cod, and range to Newfoundland in summer.

Spongomorpha sp. is a bright green tufted plant that grows 1 to 5 centimeters tall. It starts its growth attached, but is often found free-floating. It appears as rope-like masses. It is found growing on various algae in the spring, and later in the summer it is found detached. It is common from Connecticut to Newfoundland.

Bryopsis plumosa is somewhat rare around Cape Ann, but a true delight to find! It is often referred to as the Christmas tree. Plants are only a few centimeters high and are usually restricted to just below low-tide line; occasionally a few may be found in tide pools near low water. Branches of the fronds grow in only two directions, and therefore on only one plane. Healthy *Bryopsis* is dark green with evident main axes. It is found from Florida to Nova Scotia, but becomes rare north of Cape Cod.

Brown algae — phylum Phaeophyta

The cell consists of a well-defined nucleus. The inner portion of the cell wall is composed of a cellulose layer and the outer of a gelatinous layer. Alginates occur in the cell wall. The brown algae contain chlorophylls *a* and *c* (as well as xanthophylls such as fucoxanthin and diatoxanthin). The abundance of the xanthophylls is responsible for the brown color. Reproduction occurs vegetatively or sexually. Alternation of generations is common. The brown algae have the greatest size range. There are no known unicellular varieties, except the swarmers released during reproduction. Kelps on the Pacific coast are commonly 20 to 25 meters long. On our coast, they range from 6 to 7 meters long. Most species of brown algae are not this large, but rather are filamentous or aggregates of various style and complexity. The browns are flagellated during the swarmer stage. The brown algae are mostly marine. They have a wide variety of uses for man. Some use ground-up kelp instead of salt in their food. They are used directly as a rich vitamin and protein source in the diet. Algin and alginates derived from the cell wall of many brown algae have considerable value in the modern world. They are used in the processing of many paints and colorings, in smoothing and thickening dairy products such as chocolate milk and ice cream. They are used in paper products and in drugs, and in many other specific areas. They are a rich source of iodine.

Ectocarpus sp. has numerous branches. The filaments are characteristically profuse, delicate and hair-like. The plant is often attached to larger algae such as *Ascophyllum* or *Fucus*. The color is brown and can range from a few to over

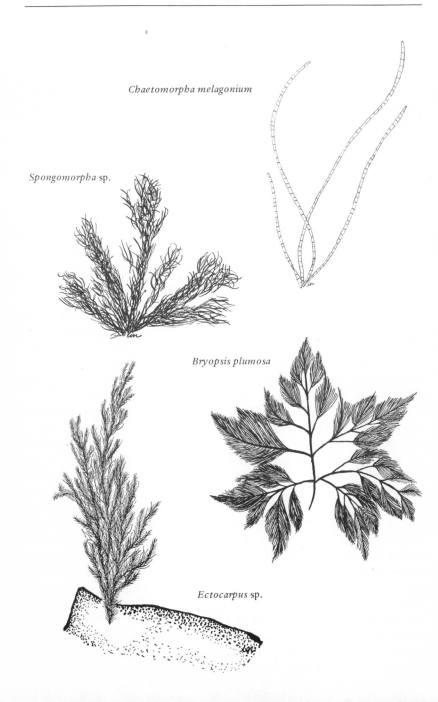

Chaetomorpha melagonium

Spongomorpha sp.

Bryopsis plumosa

Ectocarpus sp.

20 centimeters. It is common in tide pools. It fruits in early summer. Several species closely resembling each other are found in the northern New England waters.

Chordaria flagelliformis is a brown alga that grows from a disc holdfast at its base. It is deep brown in color and has sparse branching. The branches taper near their ends. The size of this plant can reach a length of 30 centimeters in the northern New England area. It is common in tide pools or in protected areas. It is found throughout the year on rocks and wood from New Jersey to northern Labrador.

Chordaria flagelliformis

Leathesia difformis is often referred to as **rat's brain** or sea potato. It is composed of spherical outgrowths that are attached usually to other algae such as Irish moss. The convoluted masses are somewhat spongy and hollow. They are filled with gas and thus very buoyant. It is olive-brown in color. About the only successful way of preserving specimens of this alga is by placing it in a container of 4 percent formalin (formaldehyde). It does not press in the conventional manner. It can be found from North Carolina to Nova Scotia in the summer.

Desmarestia viridis usually grows in deep water but often is found washed ashore. The holdfast is small but supports a system of branches covered with smaller branchlets. Growth of branches is apical. Of particular note is the acid characteristic of the cells of this alga. The sulfuric acid content is sufficiently strong to ruin all other algae in a collector's bucket within hours. It has a pH as low as 1.0. It is most abundant in early summer. This alga is yellow to light brown in color, and hair-like. It is found from New Jersey to Newfoundland.

Scytosiphon lomentaria lives in the lower tidal regions, or tide pools. It is brown in color and often about 30 centimeters in length. It grows from a small simple holdfast and is unbranched and delicate as compared to *Chorda*.

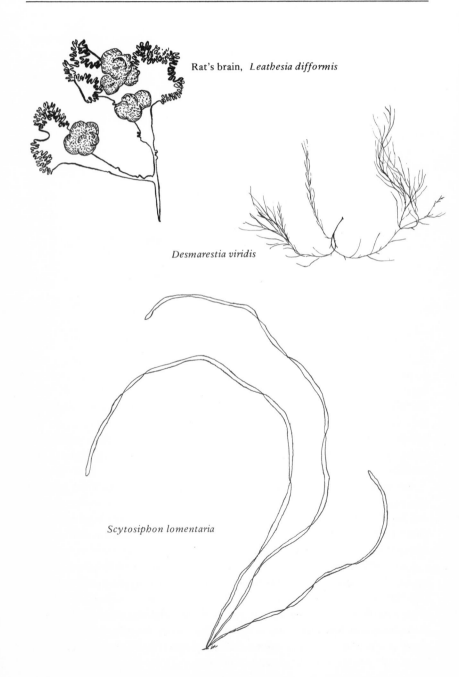

Rat's brain,   *Leathesia difformis*

Desmarestia viridis

Scytosiphon lomentaria

Dictyosiphon sp.

The plants are gregarious and found on rocks from South Carolina to northern Labrador. It is an annual which fruits from winter to late spring.

Several species of *Dictyosiphon* are in the Cape Ann area; most are quite small. They are common epiphytes. Branching is profuse and hair-like. They are brown in color, and are found from Rhode Island to Nova Scotia.

Sea whip, *Chorda filum*, resembles a long whip which can be from 10 to 70 centimeters long and is very deep brown. It grows in a long strand from a disc holdfast. It looks much like rope or cord, and hence its name. It is found in the sublittoral area or often washed ashore after heavy wave action. It ranges from New Jersey to northern Labrador.

Laminaria agardhii is commonly referred to as **kelp**. The holdfast is often branched and very tough. It has an obvious stipe and a rugged blade which is long and flat and usually unbranched. The blade has no midrib and is tapered at the end. Plants exceeding 3 meters have been found around Cape Ann. It grows below the low-tide mark or in lower tide pools. Healthy *Laminaria agardhii*, a perennial, is deep brown and found from New Jersey to Maine. Fruiting plants are normally found in winter.

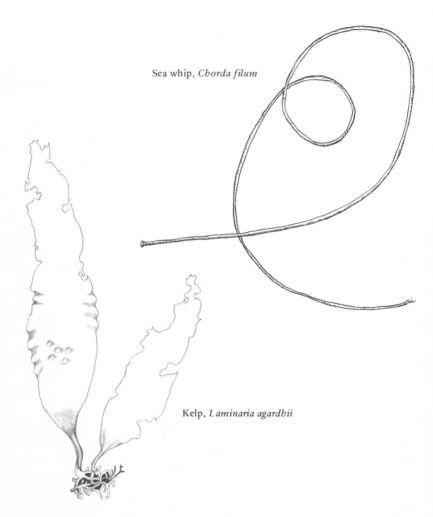

Sea whip, *Chorda filum*

Kelp, *Laminaria agardhii*

The perennial *Laminaria digitata*, **fingered kelp**, has many finger segments in the main blade. These fingers are flat and rather narrow. The plant is found locally but is less common than *Laminaria agardhii* although they grow in similar habitats. They are common north of Cape Cod and fruit in winter.

The **sea colander**, *Agarum cribrosum*, as it is known, is closely related to *Laminaria*. Its holdfast and stipe are most similar. The blade, too, is similar, except that it has an obvious midrib and is peppered with holes. Growth takes place at the base of the blade, where the holes are quite small. They increase in size toward the tip of the blade where the plant material is larger and older.

They are found in deeper water. They can grow to over a meter in length. Dwarfed forms can be found in tide pools. They occur from northern Massachusetts to Labrador.

Alaria esculenta, **winged kelp,** can reach sizes up to 3 meters. It is a perennial plant with a most obvious holdfast and unbranched stipe. The blade itself is undivided, its length greatly exceeding its width. There is an obvious midrib on the blade. Although usually restricted to the subtidal, it is frequently found washed ashore after heavy wave action. It is dark brown in color and can be found from northern Massachusetts to Labrador on rocky coasts below the tidal range.

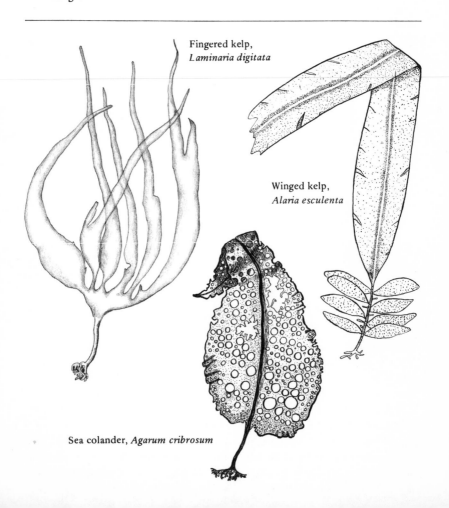

Fingered kelp,
Laminaria digitata

Winged kelp,
Alaria esculenta

Sea colander, *Agarum cribrosum*

Sea wrack, or *Fucus vesiculosus* is exceedingly abundant along the inter-tidal shores of Cape Ann. There are many species, differing mainly by re-productive structural detail. The color is a deep olive-brown and has an average length of 20 to 25 centimeters. The holdfast is small, simple and effective. Branching is dichotomous and on one plane. A midrib is conspicuous. Usually the upper blades have air bladders or floats. Other blades are tipped with reproductive structures. The floats are not reproductive, but vegetative. *Fucus* blankets the rocks between high and low tide from North Carolina to Labrador.

Knotted wrack, *Ascophyllum nodosum,* is a perennial found from New Jersey to Greenland and is one of the two most common seaweeds along the shores of Cape Ann. It shows a definite temperature response. It fruits in Long

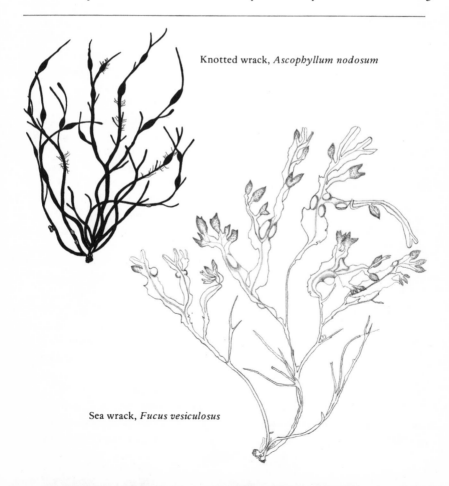

Knotted wrack, *Ascophyllum nodosum*

Sea wrack, *Fucus vesiculosus*

Island Sound in late winter or early spring; in Cape Ann in summer; and Greenland in late summer. The water temperatures at these places at these times is usually about 15°C. This alga is difficult to press due to its fleshy parts. The alga is tough and yellow-brown in color. Its average length is some 40 to 50 centimeters. The holdfast is small and simple but most effective in attaching firmly to the rocks. The main blade has short branches. There is no midrib.

Red algae — phylum Rhodophyta

The reds have a well-defined nucleus and are often multinucleate. The cell wall contains an inner layer of cellulose and an outer layer of pectic materials. Some of the walls are pitted and appear to send out protoplasmic threads to connect cells. It is not known whether there is actual communication between the cells or transmission of materials or foods. The reds contain chlorophyll *a* (as well as chlorophyll *d*, the biliproteins phycoerythrin and phycocyanin, and the carotenoid taraxanthin). The reproductive bodies are usually found on separate plants, though individual plants may contain two sex organs. The sexual plants are usually identical in form, though in some cases, the male is smaller than the female. The life cycle of many reds is very elaborate. There are few unicellular forms, most being either filamentous or undergoing apical growth or membranous sheets undergoing diffuse growth. Some of the reds are parasitic. Flagella are not present at any stage of a red alga's life. Movement of reproductive cells or unicellular forms is accomplished by floating with water currents. The reds are mostly marine, although a few occur in fresh water, especially in fast-flowing streams where there is much aeration. The reds are one of the most economically important of the algal groups. Many are used by man as food. These include *Porphyra* (nori or laver), *Rhodymenia* (dulse), and *Chondrus crispus* (Irish moss) and many more. They are used as gelatin bases, as protein-rich side dishes, as main dishes, and as vitamin sources. Red algae are also used in the production of agar-agar, fertilizers and fodder for cattle.

Nori, *Porphyra* sp., is a delicate red membranous alga which has a holdfast that is in the center of its blade. It occurs attached to other algae or directly to rocks. It is dull pink to deep red and can reach a size of 20 centimeters. Older algae may appear to be pale green. It is used as a food material in many areas of the world and is commonly referred to as nori or laver. It is found from North Carolina to Maine, and is most common in the spring.

Bonnemaisonia hamifera, previously known as *Asparagopsis,* is brilliant red in color. The lush plants branch profusely. Small hook-like branchlets occur throughout the larger branches; this is its major distinguishing characteristic.

Frequently it is dislodged from its rocky substrate and becomes entangled in other seaweeds by its small hooks. It is usually found subtidally in quite deep water. *Trailliella intricata*, a small tuft of filaments, has been found to be one of the stages in the life history of *Bonnemaisonia*.

Dumontia incrassata grows on rocks from a basal disc. It is a tubular, widely branched plant. It grows from 10 to 60 centimeters tall. It is dull red to pale yellow in appearance. It needs to be covered by water and so is found in deep tide pools and below low tide. It is most obvious in the spring from Rhode Island to Nova Scotia.

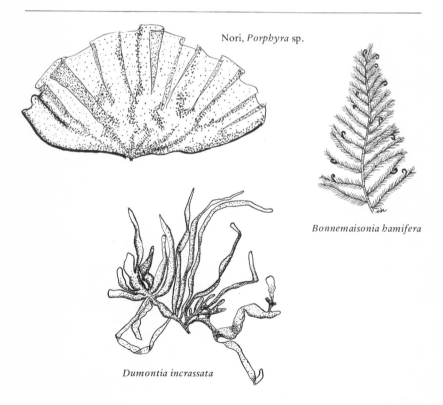

Nori, *Porphyra* sp.

Bonnemaisonia hamifera

Dumontia incrassata

Corallina officinalis with its many branches are heavily calcified ($CaCO_3$) red algae. They are flexible however, due to a lack of calcification at the joints. It is brittle and when dried, loses the pigments and appears white. It is coral-like, and small stunted plants may be found in tide pools. It is most common at low water. It is found throughout the year from Long Island to New-foundland.

Chondrus crispus, or **Irish moss** is found at the low-water line and slightly below. It is deep red in color but rapidly bleaches to green and then to white, especially the population above the low-water line. Plants exposed to strong wave action form dense mats of stunted coarse tufts. The blade does not have a midrib. A small but very strong holdfast keeps the plant attached even on the most exposed shores. The branches are all in one plane. It averages about 15 centimeters in length. It dominates the zone below *Fucus* and forms a vast mat that is as plush as a carpet. Carrageenin is extracted from it, and is used as a stabilizer in many processed foods. Many persons use this alga to congeal blancmange — a pudding. It is found throughout the year from New Jersey north.

Gigartina stellata is similar to *Chondrus* except that it has warty outgrowths on its surface and its branches curve inward toward their lower surface. It too grows from a basal disc holdfast. There is a short stipe. Branching is in a single plane. They are dark red in color and can grow 2 to 5 centimeters in length. It is much less common than *Chondrus,* but grows just above *Chondrus* in the same manner, from Rhode Island to Newfoundland.

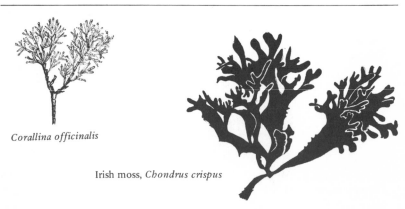

Corallina officinalis

Irish moss, *Chondrus crispus*

Rhodymenia palmata is found world-wide. **Dulse** is the common name, and it is frequently dried and eaten as a delicacy. It grows at the low-water line. It has a small basal disc, has flat blades which branch somewhat from an inconspicuous stipe. There are often many proliferations near the base. It is reddish-purple in color, and is found from New Jersey to northern Labrador throughout the year.

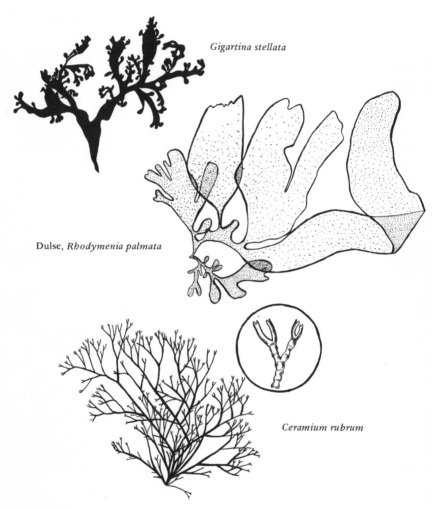

Gigartina stellata

Dulse, *Rhodymenia palmata*

Ceramium rubrum

Ceramium rubrum is frequently found among the Irish moss. It has branch-lets that end in pincers. They are finely branched with crossbars barely notice-able to the naked eye. This characteristic is the most distinguishing for classification. The color is usually deep red and this alga averages 5 to 10 centimeters in length. Many species of this genus are present on Cape Ann; however, *Ceramium rubrum* is by far the most common. It ranges from Florida to Newfoundland. It is present throughout the year and is often found on eelgrass and coarse algae.

Phycodrys rubens is pink to red in color and looks like delicate leaves. This is the only species found on the New England coast. The plant arises from a small holdfast and is stalked and lobed. There is a distinct branching system of veins. It is not common, and a treat to find. It usually grows at depths from 2 to 20 meters and it averages about 10 centimeters in length. It occurs north of Cape Cod, growing in rather deep water. It is found throughout the year.

Over 20 species of *Polysiphonia* sp. occur on the Atlantic coast from Florida north. They are red and common. Their specific identification can only be made with the aid of a microscope in most cases. *Polysiphonia lanosa* is the most common of the local species and is unique in that it grows on other algae, often *Ascophyllum*. The plant has many fine, branched filaments. It seldom is over 5 centimeters in length. They are almost brown in color, although they are red algae. It grows in the lower tidal area.

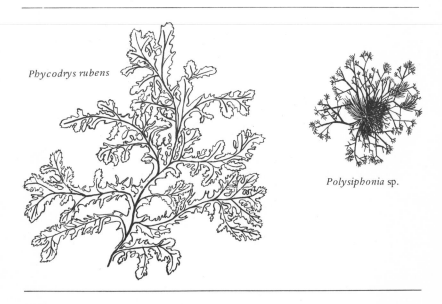

Phycodrys rubens

Polysiphonia sp.

Flowering plants

Most of the higher plants with which we are familiar are flowering plants. They are complex, with specialization of cells, tissues and organs. Flowering plants have true roots, stems and leaves. In addition, reproductive structures within the flowers are present, although not always conspicuous. In general, very few species of flowering plants are sufficiently adapted to withstand routine submersion in salt water.

Thatch grass, salt-water grass, *Spartina alterniflora,* is a tough broad-leaved grass growing stiffly upright, four or five feet tall, with alternating spikelets. Last year's stems are carried off by the tide. The plants grow so close together in the mud that little light penetrates below. This grass grows from just above mid-tide level to near the mean low-tide mark. This plant bears white flowers in August.

Fox grass, high-water cord grass, *Spartina patens,* is quite a contrast to *S. alterniflora.* This fine perennial grass, two feet high, grows from rhizomes (roots) that extend horizontally underground. The stem is rather weak, and the grass tends to bend over, giving it a tousled uncombed appearance. Last year's dead grass surrounds the roots of the new grass forming a natural

Thatch grass, *Spartina alterniflora* (tall plant) and Fox grass, *Spartina patens* (short plant)

mulch. It grows on the high marsh near the high-water mark. This plant bears dark purple flowers in August.

Spike grass, *Distichlis spicata,* is a short grass that grows in compact colonies among *Spartina patens.* It grows from rhizomes. It is a perennial and has alternate spikelets at wide intervals on the stem. These spikelets tend to curl.

Glasswort, marsh samphire, *Salicornia* sp., is a succulent plant. Both annual and perennial species are present. They have many thick-branched green stems and no apparent leaves. In the fall it turns red. It tastes strongly of salt. It was used in salads and as pickles by the early settlers. It is found on salt marshes, and sandy shores. Glasswort can tolerate salt-soaked soil in tidal areas where few plants grow. Therefore, its presence is used as an indicator of highly saline situations.

Eelgrass, *Zostera marina* is a true flowering plant that lives submerged in one to two meters of cool brackish water (less salty than normal sea water). It grows on both coasts. On the Atlantic coast, it occurs north of North Carolina. It has a creeping jointed stem with slender smooth-edged ribbon-like leaves, very narrow with blunt ends. They may be 1 to 2 meters long, and so thick that it is almost impossible to swim or wade or get a boat through it. It reproduces by seeds and from the rootstocks. The flowers are either male or female, and a plant bears one or the other — never both.

Eelgrass used to be very common all around Cape Ann. It grew so densely that it was a nuisance to swimmers and outboards at low tide. In 1931-32, a disease killed off nearly all the eelgrass on the Atlantic coast. It is now beginning to come back in several areas. Goose Cove in Annisquam is the one place on Cape Ann where the eelgrass has taken hold and re-established itself. This cove is an inlet of the Annisquam River that was bridged many years ago. The restriction of the tidal flow by the highway has resulted in a slow filling up of the cove with a muddy deposit and nearly 30 acres of eelgrass has grown up. Certain animals are found in abundance in such a stand of eelgrass.

Eelgrass has a wide geographic distribution. This is primarily due to its wide temperature tolerance. At temperatures less than $10°$ C it is dormant; from 10 to $15°$ C it grows only vegetatively; and at about $15°$ C there is flowering. Therefore, it flowers at greatly different times along the Atlantic coast. In the Cape Ann area, it blooms in July and August, while in North Carolina it blooms in March and April. This plant inhabits bays and estuaries on the Pacific and Atlantic coasts. It serves as substrate for many algal epiphytes.

Spike grass, *Distichlis spicata*

Glasswort, *Salicornia* sp.

Eelgrass, *Zostera marina*

Sea lavender, *Limonium carolinianum*, is a flowering plant that has tiny rows of lavender flowers in summer. The leaves are leathery in appearance, and occur close to the ground. They grow from one to two feet high. It is common in salt marshes in summer, occurring near glasswort.

Sea lavender, *Limonium carolinianum*

ANIMALS

Invertebrates

Sponges — phylum Porifera (the pore-bearing animals)

Sponges are very simply organized, many-celled animals. They are actually just a collection of cells, grouped around pores through which water is taken in, circulated inside the animal, and then expelled through a large vent called the osculum. Food is taken in and oxygen is absorbed as the water passes through the animal. Sponges may be single animals or colonial. They are always sessile, that is, attached to something. Sponges are found all over the world, and come in many diverse forms. They are often attached to the bottom substrate or debris, on wharf pilings, and even on the shells of crabs. Several different kinds are found around Cape Ann in varying depths of water. Two species are especially common on all the Cape Ann rocks, and one is commonly found washed ashore. The **crumb of bread sponge,** *Halichondria panicea,* is an encrusting mass of irregular form, found on rocks and stones, usually in a dark shaded spot. It is greenish or yellowish and squashy and

Crumb of bread sponge, *Halichondria panicea*

spongy to the touch. It has irregular bumps and large openings or vents, oscula, and looks rather like a moonscape. This sponge is colonial. It may be very thin in exposed areas and quite thick in sheltered spots. The thinner the sponge, the less likely it is to become loosened and torn off by wave action during a storm. It crumbles in one's hand, and has a horrid sulfur smell. It is very common at all seasons of the year in the northern Atlantic. Its range is from the Arctic Circle to southern New England.

The **eyed finger sponge,** *Haliclona oculata* occurs in upright clumps with many-branched fleshy orange-red fingers bearing prominent oscula. It is found in both shallow and deep water in the Laminarian or Kelp Zone from New

Eyed finger sponge, *Haliclona oculata*

Jersey to Labrador. The animals that live in deeper water are larger than the inshore individuals and often after a storm are found tossed up on the sandy and pebble beaches of Cape Ann. These sponges may be 30 centimeters in length and the straw yellow of the living individual soon fades to a light beige or bleaches to white when the animal dies. The more storm-battered a specimen is, the narrower the fingers are. These larger clumps are sometimes called dead man's fingers locally, although this name is usually applied to another species with a more northerly distribution and a rather palmate shape.

Polyps — phylum Coelentera (animals with a large cavity)

The polyps or coelenterates belong to an important phylum of animals because for the first time in the evolutionary ladder we find sac-like animals with radial symmetry, two layers of cells, and a definite specialization of cells. This is a diverse group containing hydromedusae, jellyfish, sea anemones, and corals. They all have two things in common: 1) an alternation of quite dissimilar generations, one attached and the other often free-swimming; and 2) the presence of nematocysts as a defense mechanism (tiny whip-like stinging cells).

Hydroids are the simplest of the coelenterates. They are a group of tiny animals usually colonial in the attached asexual or hydroid stage, and free-swimming in the sexual or medusoid stage. The hydroid forms are often found on Cape Ann rocks. These animals are very small. It is advisable to use a hand lens to appreciate the beauty of the asexual forms. When examining hydroids, the specimen should be placed in a shallow plastic dish or the cover of a plastic ice cream container, filled with sea water. Through this type of observation, in water and with a hand lens, one may often see the animals moving on the stalks or gently waving their tentacles. These tentacles containing the nematocysts are used to capture food and draw it back into the mouth. Many species of hydroids occur on Cape Ann, but there are so many that are identifiable only with a microscope that it is impractical to include them all in this guidebook. The following are some of the most common and obvious. Even these are inconspicuous animals and many of them have only Latin or scientific names.

The **club hydroid,** *Clava leptostyla,* looks like a pink encrustation on the rockweed *Ascophyllum* or on the bottom of tide pools. At first glance it appears to be a solid pincushion-shaped mass, but if you look at it with a magnifying glass, you will see that it is a colony of individual club-shaped protrusions. Sometimes they are as much as ½ centimeter in height;

Club hydroid, *Clava leptostyla* on *Ascophyllum*

each has 15-30 tentacles on top containing nematocysts. Sometimes below this cluster of tentacles, one can see a berry-like mass, which is the reproductive bud. This hydroid is common on rockweed and on stony beaches, but not on the more exposed bedrock. It is particularly abundant on Cape Ann in July and August, and is common from Long Island to Labrador.

Parasitic hydroid, *Hydractinia echinata,* a pinkish encrusting colony, is a remarkable species of hydroid that grows only on mollusk shells inhabited by living hermit crabs. Look at these animals with a magnifying glass, and several types of hydroid individuals may be seen. These are connected by a network of stolons which are actually buried in the material of the shell. There are

Hydractinia echinata, greatly enlarged

Hydractinia echinata on the shell of a hermit crab

feeding individuals (zooids) with tube-shaped bodies surrounded by tentacles. The reproductive zooids are shorter with no mouth or tentacles, but still having stinging cells at their apex. The defensive zooids surround the colony and are crowned with batteries of nematocysts. They are more slender than the others. They are quite flexible and move continuously. Found from Labrador to North Carolina, they are plentiful in the Ipswich Bay region of Cape Ann wherever there are hermit crabs. This includes sandy shores, the edge of rocks, sand and mud, and in tide pools.

Pink-hearted hydroid, *Tubularia* sp., is one of the most common colonial hydroids, several species being found on Cape Ann. Most of them range from the Bay of Fundy to southern New England. They are among the most beautiful hydroids. The pink-hearted hydroids occur in bunches of long-stemmed pink blossoms, found in tide pools and often encrusting rocks,

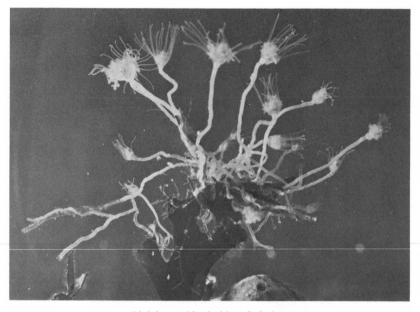

Pink-hearted hydroid, *Tubularia* sp.

pilings, floats, boat bottoms, and lobster traps. The stems are about 3 centimeters long and the blossom is 1 centimeter across. Each blossom actually is
an animal, shaped like an inverted cone, surrounded by tentacles. They are
quite flower-like. Though present all year round, these hydroids are particularly noticeable at the end of the summer when they appear on many
floating and stable objects.

Sertularia pumila is commonly found attached to seaweed or rockweed
(*Fucus*) and especially on the long fronds of kelp (*Laminaria*) in the lowest
tide pools. It also attaches itself to the sides of tide pools. It has a straight
stem up to 5 centimeters long that is bilaterally symmetrical. Members of the
colony branch off the stalk opposite each other. The tentacles emerge from
these tiny stocky branches. It is often confused with coralline algae, which
grow alongside *Sertularia* in tide pools. The alga is much heavier and coarser
and has no tentacles. It is common year round, and is found from Labrador
to Connecticut.

Jellyfish or scyphozoids are coelenterates in which the sessile stage is
small and insignificant. The free-swimming medusoid stage, the jellyfish, is
the dominant stage. This medusa is an umbrella of jelly that may be quite

Sertularia pumila

sizeable but never less than 5 centimeters in diameter. Tentacles hang down from the edge of the disc and are armed with stinging cells. A number of different jellyfish may be seen off Cape Ann, but two are particularly common.

The red or pink jellyfish or **lion's mane**, *Cyanea capillata*, is a very large animal. It may be 30 centimeters or more in diameter in Cape Ann waters, and up to 2½ meters in the northern Atlantic. The edge of the umbrella is scalloped into 8 lobes, each of which is subdivided until there are 32 indentations. A great many long tentacles hang down from this edge. This edge is quite delicate in contrast to the thick gelatinous center of the animal. Each tentacle carries stinging cells, which are so numerous that a swimmer who accidentally touches this animal may be seriously stung. The lion's mane was used as a murder weapon in one of the Sherlock Holmes stories. Below the center of the disc, inside the tentacles, are the lobes of the stomach, the stomach pouches and the gonads. The powerful muscle that rhythmically

Lion's mane or pink jellyfish, *Cyanea capillata*

contracts the umbrella is a dark brown color. Sometimes these jellyfish appear off Cape Ann in quantity. Sometimes none or only a few are present in late June and July. In August and September they are found off the coast of Maine. They range around the northern Atlantic to Scandinavia.

The **moonjelly**, *Aurelia aurita,* is the common white or translucent jellyfish that often covers Cape Ann beaches and swims offshore in July and August. Its disc is 18 to 30 centimeters in diameter. Like *Cyanea,* the disc is firm and gelatinous in the center, tapering off to a delicate edge fringed with short tentacles. The tissue of the jellyfish is transparent and the four-sided mouth can be seen. This tapers off into four mouth arms which are rather stiff and gelatinous, hanging below the umbrella. Four gonads may be seen from above. The male gonads are pale pink and the female gonads are white. It ranges from Greenland to the West Indies.

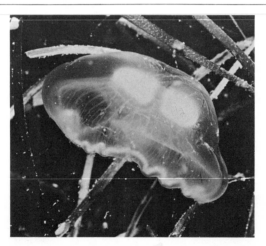

Moonjelly, *Aurelia aurita*

Sea anemones, anthozoa, (flower-like animals) are characterized by high contractible cylindrical bodies with radiating tentacles surrounding the mouth at the top of the cylinder. The bottom of the cylinder is a basal disc with which the animal attaches itself to the substrate, usually something substantial like rock, wharf pilings or shells. A sea anemone can move by extending a portion of this basal disc and attaching, then contracting it, thus pulling itself into a new position. Reproduction occurs by ripening of sperm and egg cells. This occurs at different times in one individual. They are expelled into the water and fertilization occurs by chance. Anemones also reproduce asexually. One often finds a large anemone surrounded by smaller ones. These have been formed by pedal laceration, a process whereby new individuals grow from bits torn off the pedal disc of the larger anemone.

The **common sea anemone,** *Metridium dianthus,* is the species found on all the rocky shores of Cape Ann, from lower tide pools down into the Kelp Zone in ocean and harbor. A beautiful creature, it sometimes looks more like a plant than an animal when all of its tentacles are extended. It may have up to 1000 tentacles. The stout cylindrical body may be white, orange, chocolate-brown or an intermediate tan color. It may be firm, erect, and bearing tentacles, or the tentacles may be contracted, giving the animal a bulgy tomato-like shape. The animal may be so contracted that it is like a dark smear on the rock. The sea anemone uses its tentacles to grab food. It consumes particles of live or dead material as large as a small fish. The poison in the nematocysts immediately kills whatever victim is caught, but it is harmless to man. It is usually found in colonies of 20 to 100 individuals, though as few as 4 or 5 large individuals may be found together. This sea anemone likes dark places under overhanging rocks protected from the light by dangling seaweed at low tide. It is occasionally found out of the water for a very short time, but generally it is submerged. This species moves about, and a large colony of one summer may completely relocate itself during the winter. It is found at all seasons.

Common sea anemone, *Metridium dianthus*

Comb jellies — phylum Ctenophora, (comb-bearing animals)

Comb jellies are small gelatinous animals superficially resembling jellyfish. However, they are actually quite different, having a distinct biradial (having both bilateral and radial) symmetry, no alternation of generations, and no nematocysts or stinging cells on their tentacles. Most ctenophores are round. Some are spherical, some helmet-shaped, and a few are flattened. All have 8 rows of nearly transparent comb-plates, radiating like lines of longitude on a globe at equally-spaced intervals running from the mouth on top to the bottom. These comb-plates are covered with tiny hairs and are continually beating at a fast rate, creating a current, and moving the animal through the water. Unlike the jellyfish, which move with their mouths underneath and behind, the comb jelly advances mouth first. Some species have long tentacles which are carried contracted and coiled up inside or extended to trail behind. The tentacles are covered with a sticky substance which catches the tiny plankton that is the food supply for the animal. Although comb jellies are able to propel themselves in the water, they are actually plankton. Therefore, the ocean currents determine their distribution. Occasionally, they appear in large numbers off the New England coast. Their gelatinous bodies are so clear they are often not observed in the water, and only noticed when cast up on a beach or into a shallow tide pool. They may occur at any time of the year, and several species may be found. The sea walnut is perhaps the most common.

The **sea walnut,** *Pleurobrachia pileus,* is occasionally found along Cape Ann shores. It is a clear, slightly flattened, spherical animal sometimes tinged milky white or brownish-orange-yellow on the tentacles. It has 8 distinct rows of comb-plates, running like lines of longitude from top to bottom. About 2 centimeters in diameter, it is quite conspicuous when washed up on a beach. Sometimes the entire edge of the beach is glistening with reflections from the bodies of these little animals. It is more visible on the background of the sand than in the water. The tentacles may be contracted and not visible, or may be trailing behind. Put one of the animals in a plastic container and look at it with a hand lens. The comb-plates may be seen as a blur, that is, violently moving back and forth so that a continuous ripple seems to be moving around each of the 8 bands of comb-plates around the animal. In certain light, this produces a very beautiful iridescent effect. *Pleurobrachia pileus* may occur from Cape Cod to eastern Canada, being much more common off Cape Ann and in the colder waters.

Sea walnut comb jelly, *Pleurobrachia pileus*

Flatworms — phylum Platyhelminthes

Flatworms are soft, unsegmented, flat animals with no appendages. They are the first group in the evolutionary sense, to have bilateral symmetry. They have a definite anterior (front end), recognizable by behavior, but no distinctly separated head. The digestive cavity of the flatworm is primitive. Like that of the coelenterates, it is sac-like, and the mouth serves both to take in food and discharge waste. Most flatworms are parasitic, but there is an important group of these worms that are marine free-living creatures called turbellarians (class Turbellaria) from the Latin word for turbulence. The skin of these animals is heavily ciliated on the underside, that is, the skin is covered with tiny hairs that are continually moving and make a swirly turbulence which can only be seen under the microscope. There are many species of these to be found in intertidal waters, most very small and difficult to identify. One species, however, is very common under rocks and tide pools on Cape Ann.

Notoplana atomata (formerly called *Leptoplana variabilis*) is a highly variable little worm. About 3 centimeters long, it has a narrow oblong body. There are no tentacles, but 4 conspicuous eye clusters are on the anterior part of the body, and a mouth is on the ventral or underside. It may be yellowish

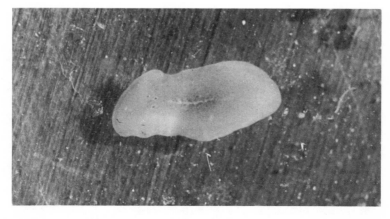

Notoplana atomata

brown to a light salmon color, often with orange-brown spots. It may blend in with its background. When you turn over a rock, this animal may be sticking tightly to the rock surface; it may be on the bottom of a tide pool. If removed and placed in salt water in a small plastic dish, its undulating swimming motions may be observed. Very common from Cape Cod north, this animal is found all around the northern Atlantic to Scandinavia.

Ribbon worms — phylum Nemertea

Nemertean worms belong to the phylum Nemertea. They are a group of soft-bodied, very contractile, cylindrical to flattened animals which are unsegmented externally. The mouth opens into a straight digestive tube which ends in an anus at the rear or posterior end of the animal. This is a step up from the flat worms that have no anus at all. Nemerteans are armed with a proboscis, an organ of defense which also captures prey and helps the animal burrow in the sand, but has nothing to do with the digestive system — that is, it is not the actual mouth of the animal. The proboscis originates in an opening near the mouth and may be turned inside out. It is often armed with stout spines, and may extend a long way. When handled, these worms can break up into several pieces, which continue to live independently and can regenerate lost parts.

Cerebratulus lacteus is the largest of American shallow-water nemerteans. It can grow up to 6 meters long and 2 or 3 centimeters wide. It is nocturnal, swims at night, and burrows in the sand and mud near low-water mark

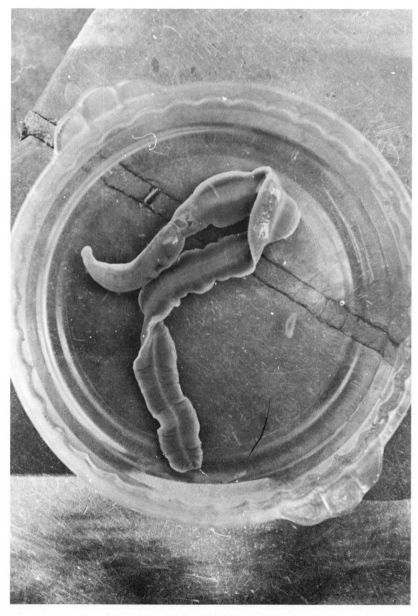

Cerebratulus lacteus

during the day. It is a smooth, cream or flesh-colored worm with a blunt triangular head. It has no eyespots, but has cephalic slits, which are long and deep, and run the length of the head. These slits are lined with red, and the red lateral nerve trunk shows through the edge of the whole body, which is fin-like on each side, and extremely well-adapted for swimming. The mouth is a long narrow slit on the ventral side of the head. The proboscis is everted through a large terminal proboscis pore. In large specimens, the proboscis may reach 1 meter when extended. It is found from Maine to North Carolina and is common in the Annisquam River area.

True or segmented worms — phylum Annelida (the ringed animals)

Segmented worms are bilaterally symmetrical animals with a digestive track which runs longitudinally from mouth to anus. This digestive tract is situated in a true body cavity, a coelom. Elongated bodies divided into a number of segments are characteristic of the annelids. They have a definite head region which is sometimes made up of distinct segments, sometimes of fused segments, but always bearing organs adapted to a head region, such as those used for grabbing, tearing, tasting, and seeing, as well as a so-called brain. The rest of the segments are identical in structure except the last one, which contains the anus. All marine annelids have on each segment a pair of lateral appendages called parapodia, which generally are two-lobed. Bunches of bristles or setae extend from each of these lobes and are of various forms: jointed, feathery, serrated, or stalked with paddles for swimming. The marine annelids are in one class called Polychaeta, meaning many hairs. The poly-chaetes are adapted to various environments in the intertidal area. Some crawlers live in mud and sand under rocks or in holdfasts of kelp and among the byssal threads of mussels. Others build tubes and attach themselves to rocks and other firm substrates or make burrows in the sand.

The **scaleworm**, *Lepidonotus squamatus,* is the most common annelid worm of the rocky shore. Look carefully under stones, in crevices of tide pools, in the interstices between mussels, barnacles, sea squirts and encrust-ing algae and hydroids and you will find a stout little worm up to 3 centi-meters in length and covered with 12 pairs of scales, elytra, that overlap like shingles from head to tail. Each scale is covered with rough granules that may be seen with a hand lens, as may the bunches of setae or bristles that extend out from each side. The color of this animal is variable — brownish, tannish, reddish or greenish — with or without a row of darker spots. This scale worm is found in the northern Atlantic and northern Pacific, but is not

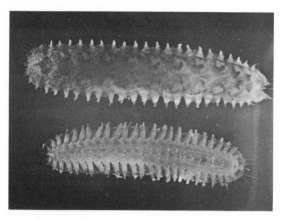

Scaleworm, *Lepidonotus squamatus*

an Arctic form. In the United States, it ranges from the Gulf of St. Lawrence to New Jersey, and from Alaska to Mexico.

Harmothoë imbricata is another scale worm and one of the most common found on rocky shores in northern waters, being an Arctic, Pacific and Atlantic species, ranging on the east coast from Long Island, New York, north. It is found intertidally as well as in deeper water on rough stones, in tide pools, with sponge, on holdfasts of kelp and in the byssal threads of mussels. About 6 centimeters long, the animal has 37 segments with bristly setae on each side. It has various colors — grays, browns, blacks and greens with a speckled and mottled pattern.

The **clam worm**, *Nereis virens* (or *Neanthes virens*) is a large handsome bright iridescent marine annelid strongly marked with a blue line down the middle of the ventral side and dark bristles or parapodia. It may be up to 50 centimeters long. It may be found in mud or sand in sheltered bays and marshlands, but is more commonly found in the sand. It constructs a tube with a sticky fluid that is excreted from glands located along its body. The tube formed by the hardening of this fluid is flexible and covered with grains of sand. The worm fits tightly into this tube, and can move in and out very fast and at will. A good swimmer, *Nereis* comes out of its tube at night to hunt. It has a large proboscis armed with powerful pincer claws with which it catches worms and other animals. The clam worm is sold extensively as bait and many a fisherman has had his fingers nipped when putting clam worms on the hooks. It ranges from Labrador to southern New England. It is found in the mud all around Cape Ann.

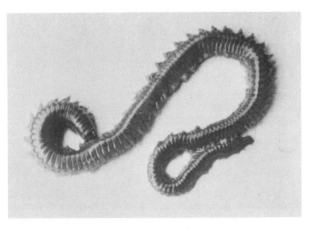

Clam worm, *Nereis* sp.

Nereis pelagica is the **clam worm** of the rocky shore. It is smaller, the largest being only 21 centimeters long, but similar to the clam worm *Nereis virens,* which is so extensively used as bait. The name clam worm is a misnomer. The worm has nothing to do with a clam, other than occasionally being found in a dead clam or mussel shell. These worms are found intertidally on rocky shores, under rocks and in crevices, among the byssal threads of mussels, in sponges, and in the holdfasts of various kelps. They are particularly apt to creep under the red encrusting algae on the bottom of tide pools. These are spectacular worms of an iridescent brownish-green color, and are always found in clean circulating water — therefore, in tide pools in the Irish Moss Zone or lower down. Most of this worm's life is spent on the bottom except when it is sexually mature. Then it swims up to the surface waters. It eats algae (sea lettuce, *Ulva*), and many kinds of marine life, including other worms. It has been found in the stomachs of cod and haddock. *Nereis pelagica* can be distinguished from *Nereis virens* by a difference in arrangement of the bristles observable only under a microscope, or by its habitat. It lives on rocky shores from Greenland to Virginia.

The **coiled worms,** *Spirorbis borealis,* are tiny snail-like worms that live in coiled calcareous tubes which they attach to seaweed, rockweed or Irish moss, and sometimes to the shells of mussels, snails and other mollusks. They are very numerous and often the seaweed is flecked with white, as if spattered by paint. Look at a coiled worm tube carefully with a magnifying glass. The opening of the tube is about ½ millimeter in diameter, and the entire tube is only 1 millimeter across. Many of these are dead, empty shells, but occasionally at an extremely low tide, they can be found alive. Examine the live coiled worm in water, and look for the wreath of tentacles. On one side, there is a plug on the end of a stalk which is the operculum. The operculum fits into the mouth of the tube when the animal is contracted into its tube, and makes an airtight door so that there is no danger of the coiled worm drying out when it is out of water at low tides. It is common all around Cape Ann.

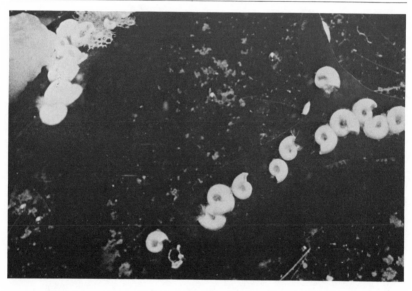

Coiled worm, *Spirorbis borealis*

The **blood worm** or beak thrower, *Glycera dibranchiata,* is a large (18 to 25 centimeters) purplish-pink worm with a pink line running along its back for its entire length, and has very fine pink bristles or parapodia seen with a hand lens. It has a small sharp-pointed head and a large evertible sac which, when turned inside out, resembles a club-like proboscis armed with four curved black hooks which can give a sharp bite. When free-swimming, it moves in a spiral manner. It can disappear quickly in the sand by corkscrewing its way out of sight. It has no blood vessels, but the cavity between the gut and the skin is filled with red blood, hence its name. It is often sold for bait. It ranges from Massachusetts to Charleston, South Carolina.

The trumpet worm or **mason worm,** *Cistenides gouldii,* is a remarkable

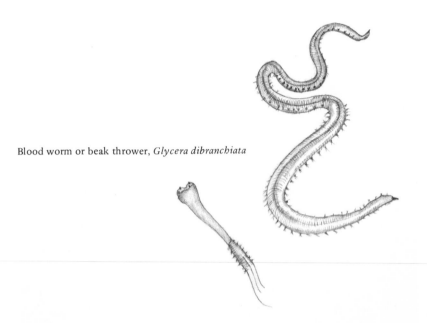

Blood worm or beak thrower, *Glycera dibranchiata*

annelid that constructs a tapering tube out of sand grains. Each is fitted as
neatly as a stone in a dry wall. The sand grains are cemented together with
smaller grains at the small end of the tube and larger sizes at the larger end.
The worm has an obliquely-truncated head which it can extend from the large
end of the tube. The head is surrounded by two long antennae and a semi-
circle of fringing papillae (small fleshy protuberances) in front and two sets of
golden bristles (setae) which look like combs and are used to dig a burrow
in the sand and to put sand into the mouth. This worm lives upside down
(head downwards) in sand with the small end of the tube extending up into the
water and eats by passing sand through itself and extracting food from the inter-
stitial spaces, the area between sand grains. It lives from low-water mark to 20
meters, from Maine to North Carolina. It lives all around Cape Ann on sheltered
sandy beaches and also in sandy places between rocks on boulder or pebble
beaches. The tiny sand tubes are sometimes washed ashore.

The **bamboo worm** or jointed worm, *Clymenella torquata*, is a brick-red
slender worm made up of a number of segments that have bright red bands
around the swollen parts of the rings. The name bamboo worm comes from the
fact that like the plant, each segment is longer than it is wide. A good field
mark! The fifth ring of the bamboo worm is always a peculiar color and marks
this species which has a curious caudal appendage on its tail, a funnel-shaped

Trumpet worm or mason worm, *Cistenides gouldii*

structure surrounded by small fleshy appendages. There are two color phases of this worm: one, pale with red nodes; and when in mud, it is green. The last 3 rings have no bristles. This worm builds a neat straight tube of mucus and fine sand. It is found in sheltered sandy areas such as the Annisquam River section of Cape Ann, from the Bay of Fundy to New Jersey.

Crustaceans, spiders and insects — phylum Arthropoda
(the joint-footed animals)

The arthropods are characterized by a hard exoskeleton, external segmentation, and jointed appendages. Because insects are arthropods, this group contains a larger number of species than all the other groups together. Unlike the annelids, the segments of the arthropods differ greatly in size, shape, and number. The jointed appendages are adapted to various uses: grabbing, crushing, crawl-

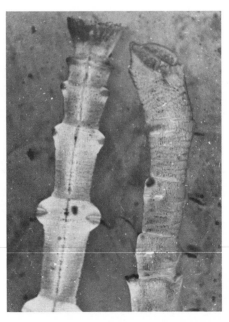

Bamboo worm or jointed worm, *Clymenella torquata*

ing, walking or flying. The sexes are separate. The eggs develop into larvae which go through several distinct stages before they reach the adult form. Because of the hard exoskeleton, arthropods must shed their outside skins to grow. Often the old skeletons of crabs, lobsters, barnacles, and other crustaceans are found at the edge of the tide. The crustaceans are one of the classes of arthropods, and include crabs, lobsters, shrimps and water fleas. Another class, the insects (a huge and mostly terrestrial class) has one marine representative found on the rocky shores of Cape Ann, *Anurida*.

Barnacles are the most common crustaceans found on Cape Ann. They are magnificently adapted to the place they live — the bare rocks which are pounded mercilessly by ocean waves at all seasons of the year. They can stand more extremes of exposure than any other animal that occurs on the New England coast — heat of summer, freezing cold of winter, and tons of pressure from wave action. By means of secreting a cement, they anchor themselves to rock or any underwater bare area such as undersides of boats, pilings or shells. The barnacle has reduced itself to the bare necessities of life. In the larval stage, it is free-swimming, and is bilaterally symmetrical with a head, body, and paired appendages. As soon as it becomes adult, it swims below the surface of the water, and attaches itself headfirst to the first firm object it encounters. There it secretes a limy shell and its body form is reduced to a mouth, a digestive tract and its six pairs of legs, which lie on top and are extendible outside the shell when the upper plates are separated. These legs continually move when extended and force a current of water into their mouths, from which food and oxygen are extracted. Barnacles are bisexual. They cross-fertilize; therefore it is of much advantage for the animals to live in close contact. Barnacles live all over the world and come in many different forms. The rock barnacles are common on the New England coast. Two species of these are found on the rocky shores of Cape Ann.

The **common rock barnacle,** *Balanus balanoides,* has a small cone-shaped shell less than 2 centimeters in diameter, very rough on the outside, made up of several limey plates that do not come together in a point, but stop like the crater of a volcano. Across this hole is a lid made up of four small sections

Rock barnacle, *Balanus* sp.

of shell arranged so that they can open up to let the feet emerge. At low tide look for feeding barnacles in upper tide pools, and for closed, resting barnacles in the Barnacle Zone, where they thickly encrust the rocks, crowding closely ✓ together. The edges of the vertical shells are quite sharp. When out of water at low tide, the upper plates of the barnacle close tightly and prevent the animal from drying out in the air. This animal has a membranous base which can be scraped off the rocks. It ranges from the Arctic Ocean to Delaware Bay.

The **large rock barnacle,** *Balanus balanus,* is a very large species up to 3 centimeters, that lives lower down the intertidal zone than the common rock barnacle. It has rough dirty-white wall plates that are strongly ribbed with long square longitudinal tubes and a calcareous base. The upper sections fit together in a different pattern from the common rock barnacle. The large rock barnacle is common north of Cape Cod well into Arctic waters.

The division of crustacean arthropods, Isopoda, includes animals with legs of equal length. They are bilaterally symmetrical and somewhat flattened from back to front. They have body segmentation and a pair of legs on each of the thoracic or chest segments, usually 7. They have a pair of pleopods, swimming and breathing organs, off each abdominal segment. On the head there is found a pair of eyes, 2 pairs of antennae, and hard and soft jaws. They are small and a hand lens is necessary to examine them in detail. There are a great many different species of isopods occurring on Cape Ann. Most are difficult to identify without using an elaborate key. Like most crustaceans, isopods are scavengers and are found wherever there is decaying animal matter. Two species, however, are very common in the tide pools and in the Irish Moss Zone on Cape Ann.

Idotea baltica is a large isopod. The male may grow to 3 centimeters in length. It is dark green in color, though this may vary. The abdomen is more than one-third of the entire body. It has large compound eyes located at the extreme margin of the head. There are 3 pairs of thoracic legs somewhat hooked at the end, and 4 pairs of abdominal legs and a large tail, a telson, ending in a three-toothed or shield-shaped plate. From the Gulf of St. Lawrence to North Carolina, it can be found at the edge of the water, on floating seaweed and on seaweed growing on rocks.

Idotea phosphorea is a conspicuous isopod found in tide pools and in the Irish Moss Zone of the rocky shore of Cape Ann. It is about 3 centimeters in length and its telson or tail plate ends in one sharp point. The head is broader than long, and its eyes are located at the extreme anterior edges. It is dark

Isopod, *Idotea baltica*

green or brown with prominent patches of yellow or white. The range of this animal is from the Gulf of St. Lawrence to New Haven, Connecticut.

Sand hoppers, beach fleas, gammarids and caprellids, are amphipods, animals with two different kinds of legs. Amphipoda are small crustaceans that are generally flattened from side to side and have an arched appearance due to the strong curve of the body segments. The head segment is often fused with the 7 thoracic segments and the abdominal segments are sometimes compressed. The gills are on the first joints of the thoracic legs on the underside. The eye is always sessile, that is, never on a stalk. They have 2 antennae and 5 pairs of thoracic walking legs followed by 3 pairs of abdominal legs adapted for swimming. The last 3 pairs of abdominal appendages are stiff and used for jumping. These animals swim, walk, or jump upon their sides. There are many amphipods living among the seaweed cast upon the beaches or rocks at the strand line. Most belong to a special group called gammarids. Gammarids are amphipods that are numerous in the tide pools, under rocks, and among the intertidal seaweeds of Cape Ann. Like the isopods, a special key is needed to determine the species. Any small (up to 3 centimeters in length) red, brown or greenish laterally flattened animals with small heads and eyes, and strongly-arched backs should be looked up in a special key. Sometimes a tide pool will be full of them swimming around. If you swish the kelp around, hundreds will appear in the water all over your hand and arm. Turn over rocks, and the area exposed will be swarming with little dark red creatures, some quite large with small ones attached. These are the males and females. The females are the larger. In northern polar waters these gammarids are so numerous that a ship-wrecked group once survived on them alone for four months.

A gammarid amphipod

The caprellids are another group of amphipods. They have a very long segmented body and move about the seaweed like an inchworm. They are tiny. Males are about 2 centimeters and females are smaller. A hand lens is necessary to appreciate the unique appearance of these creatures. They are something like an animated jointed toothpick. In the spring, the females carry their eggs internally in a transparent egg sac. They live low down in the Irish Moss Zone and at a very low tide the whole mass of seaweed is alive with the caprellids inching their way around in search of food. They assume the color of whatever they are near and are hard to see until they move. Common from Greenland south to Long Island they can be found on the sheltered rocks of Cape Ann.

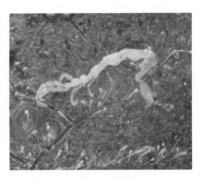

A caprellid amphipod

Shrimp, lobsters, crabs are decapods, animals with 10 legs. These crustaceans, the decapods, are characterized by a carapace which covers all the
thoracic segments, including the head. They have a pincer and a crusher
claw and 4 pairs of walking legs in the thoracic region, and paired swimmerettes or pleopods under the abdomen. The gills are found under the
carapace branching either from the base of the legs or from the body wall.
The sexes are distinguished by the specialization of the first pair of abdominal
swimmerettes into a horn-like sperm depositor in the male or into soft and
underdeveloped flabby swimmerettes in the female. The sperm is retained
by the female for a long time, and the eggs are fertilized as they emerge over
the stored sperm. The eggs are carried adhered to the female swimmerettes
until they hatch. A decapod with an egg mass is said to be in berry.

Shrimp — the pink or **deep sea shrimp**, *Pandalus borealis*, occur in large
numbers off Cape Ann, but only in water over 100 meters deep, and are
rarely found washed up on the shore. Other shrimp inhabit warmer waters.

The **sand shrimp**, *Crangon septemspinosus*, is a true decapod and occurs
abundantly on all the sandy and muddy shores of Cape Ann, and occasionally
even in tide pools. It is completely camouflaged on sand and one has to look
twice to distinguish its outline. Sometimes one is only aware of it as it tickles
one's toes when standing at the edge of low tide on a sandy beach. It is translucent, pale gray in color, with tiny dark spots. It has long antennae, and
when examined closely with a hand lens, one can see that the legs have claws
and that there is a dorsal spine posterior to (back of) the rostrum, that part
of the shell that extends out over the mouth. Some subspecies have several
dorsal spines. These animals are hard to catch because they move very rapidly

Deep sea shrimp, *Pandalus borealis*

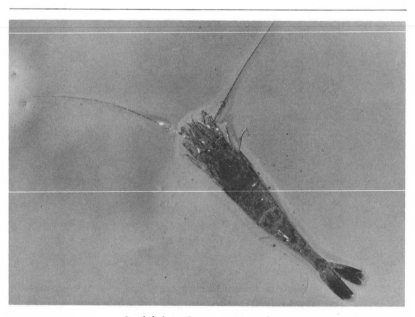

Sand shrimp, *Crangon septemspinosus*

in an unexpected direction with a quick flick of the tail which propels them backwards. These shrimp are eaten by many kinds of fish. They reproduce at a rapid rate and therefore easily maintain their numbers. They range from Labrador to North Carolina.

The **American lobster,** *Homarus americanus,* was once the most common large crustacean on Cape Ann, and could be found in all the lowest tide pools. Extensively caught by lobstermen with traps and pursued by SCUBA divers with their hands, the number of lobsters has been drastically reduced. Occasionally in June or July, one can be found that has recently shed its shell. It is illegal to take a lobster without a license. A legal lobster in Massachusetts has a carapace " more than 3 and 3/16 inches" (8 centimeters) from the eye socket to the posterior (back) edge. If you find a lobster, catch it, look at it carefully, but be sure to release it promptly.

The lobster has 10 thoracic legs, 4 pairs of walking legs, and a forward or anterior pair equipped with enormous pincer and crusher claws. It is dark green, blotched with blue and reddish markings, much darker on top and a light yellowish color underneath. A lethargic animal, it likes to back into a crevice well-hidden by seaweed and stay there all day. At night it walks around the bottom scavenging and feeding on dead material. When threatened, the lobster puts up its claws like a prizefighter, but prefers to move rapidly away from danger by a flip of its powerful abdomen (not to be confused with a tail) and moves backward.

Lobsters grow slowly, casting their shells some 25 times before they get to legal size, which takes about 5 years. Their size varies considerably. Offshore

American lobster, *Homarus americanus*

lobsters of more than 23 kilograms have been taken in very deep water. The average inshore lobster is about 30 centimeters long, and weighs about 0.7 kilograms. There is an apparent migration of lobsters. Sonic tags attached to lobsters have revealed that the lobsters themselves do not migrate, but become dormant as they are surrounded by cold water. They are active and trapped where the water is warmest. Offshore waters warm prior to inshore waters. Lobsters are therefore noted offshore in early June and inshore in July and August. As temperature decreases again, lobsters are only noted offshore.

Hermit crabs are found all around Cape Ann, on rocky and sandy shores and on the muddy bottoms of the marshes. There are two different species, much alike except for size. All hermit crabs occupy the empty shells of marine snails, gastropods, instead of having a complete hard exoskeleton like other arthropods. They are decapods like the lobster and shrimp, but are adapted to fit into a coiled snail shell. Two pairs of walking legs, large pincer and grabbing claws are extendible outside the lip of the shell. The rest of the hermit crab is in the form of the letter C. The fourth and fifth pairs of legs are attached to the chest or cephalothorax, and are much reduced in length. At the base of the telson, a pair of swimmerettes or uropods are modified to act as anchors in the columella of the snail. The hermit crab wedges itself so tightly in its chosen shell that it is almost impossible to pull it out alive without tearing these uropods. Hermit crabs grow as do other arthropods, splitting their skins (which are very thin) and then moving into a larger snail's shell. Often when looking into a tide pool, one is astonished to see a snail moving at quite a fast clip; upon investigation the shell will prove to be inhabited by a hermit crab.

Pagurus pollicaris is the large reddish-brown crab that inhabits medium-deep water and is often found cast up on the beach or pulled up in lobster pots. It lives in large shells such as the moon snail, *Lunatia heros,* and the waved whelk, *Buccinum undatum.* It is easily identified by its large, broad and rather flat crusher and pincer claws that are covered with small tubercules. The 2 pairs of walking legs are much narrower than the big claws and the other 2 pairs of legs are not visible unless the animal is out of its shell. When withdrawn into its shell, this hermit crab can block the aperture so tightly that it is possible for the animal to be stranded on land between tides without drying out. *Pagurus pollicaris* is more common on sandy beaches than off rocks. They cannot withstand being rolled in the surf and crashed on hard granite. Therefore, look for them in the Ipswich Bay area off the beaches, in the Annisquam River or off rocks in the more sheltered parts of Gloucester Harbor. They range and are quite common from Maine to Florida.

Hermit crab, *Pagurus pollicaris*

Pagurus longicarpus is the small hermit crab found in the shells of peri-winkles, *Littorina* sp.; dog whelks, *Thais lapillus;* and nassa mud snails, *Nassarius* sp. One will find these all around Cape Ann. Like the larger hermits, *Pagurus longicarpus* is a dark rosy color. It has very sharp pincer and crusher claws and quite long spidery walking legs. On examination with a hand lens, tiny eyes can be seen at the ends of the eyestalks. These very active busy little crabs are interesting to watch as they scramble around the tide pools, sometimes trying to pull one another out of their shells.

True crabs are quite different in shape from the shrimps and lobsters. They are decapods having 10 thoracic legs but the carapace at the back of the crab is short and broad in contrast to the long narrow cephalothorax of the lobster. The abdomen, which in the lobster provides such good eating, and is mistak-enly called the tail, is much reduced in size. The abdomen is tucked under the ventral side of the carapace, which has an inverted groove to receive it. The

Small hermit crab, *Pagurus longicarpus* in a common periwinkle

dorsal side of the abdomen lies flush with the ventral surface of the carapace. The shape of the abdomen indicates the sex of the crab. A male crab has an abdomen shaped like an isosceles triangle, while the female has a broader equilaterally-shaped abdomen. By carefully pulling out the abdomen so that the swimmerettes (uropods) are exposed, one can see that they are modified like the lobster's. The first pair is modified into a hard sperm-depositor in the male, while the female has a number of soft uropods adapted to holding the egg mass under the abdomen. In the late spring, one often finds a crab with an orange-yellow mass bulging out from under the abdomen — this is the egg mass. These are pregnant females which should be returned to the water and released immediately.

The 10 legs of the true crabs are subdivided into 4 pairs of walking legs and a pincer and crusher claw. In some species, the last pair is adapted to swimming by having a paddle shape instead of being pointed. Like lobsters, crabs are scavengers and move about at the base of seaweed or along the bottom, eating whatever dead material they can find. There are 3 kinds of crabs commonly found on Cape Ann rocks and one, a toad crab, occurs just offshore.

The **common rock crab**, *Cancer irroratus,* can be found all summer along the rocky shores of Cape Ann on the seaward side and in the harbors in tide pools. With the aid of a mask and snorkel, they can be seen on the banks of Irish moss and deeper among the holdfasts of kelp. In winter as the temperature drops, the crabs appear to move out into much deeper water. Cast carapaces of this type of crab are commonly found on the strand line of sand and rocks. The color of a live rock crab is yellow-red. The forward edge of the carapace is crenulated with smooth protuberances or teeth running from the eyes to the outer edge of the shell, which is almost as wide as it is deep, suggesting a capital D.

Common rock crab, *Cancer irroratus*

The **Jonah crab**, *Cancer borealis,* is similar to the rock crab, but is more of a deep purple color. The indentations on the forward part of the shell are rougher than on the common rock crab with almost a tooth-on-tooth arrangement. The whole animal is more massive, with heavier claws. The crusher and pincer claws are tipped with black. The Jonah crab is more lethargic than the rock crab, but otherwise has similar habits. When the cast shells are found on the strand line or elsewhere, they are red, the color a lobster turns when cooked. The exoskeleton of all the marine crustaceans turns red after death, no matter what color it was to begin with, or how it died.

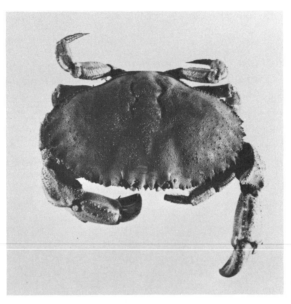

Jonah crab, *Cancer borealis*

The **little green crab,** *Carcinus maenas,* is found all around Cape Ann: in the seaweed, under rocks, in tide pools, and in the salt marshes. They are very numerous, although not conspicuous in daylight unless you hunt for them. At night they are everywhere. Go to a tide pool or exposed areas of seaweed with a flashlight after dark, and you will see countless little green crabs scuttling about their business. They are active creatures, well-named after the maenads, the frenzied Greek bacchantes. A dark blue-green in color, this crab has a square-like carapace in contrast to its long walking legs and narrow pincer and crusher claws. They are scavengers that are constantly exploring the holdfast of sea-weeds for decaying matter and will be found feeding freely on any dead fish or other such material. The shells are cast frequently, and the casts are often found before the crab itself. Actually classed with swimming crabs, the little green crab is different from the edible blue crab, not only in color and shape of carapace, but in having a pointed terminal segment on the last pair of walking legs, instead of a paddle.

The **toad crabs,** *Hyas coarctatus,* are deep-water crabs, not often found on the rocky shore of Cape Ann. They are taken in the nets of draggers in water 30 meters or more in depth, occasionally found in the stomachs of cod, and a small one sometimes appears in the deeper tide pools of the Kelp Zone. The

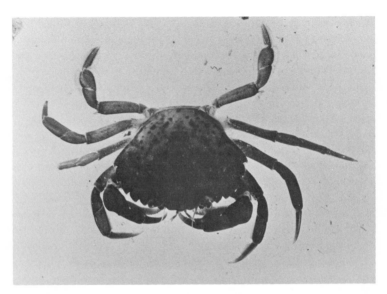

Little green crab, *Carcinus maenas*

Toad crab, *Hyas coarctatus*

carapace is long and narrow, and has indentations on the side, which make it resemble a cello or violin. The legs are all about the same length, and are short and compact. The entire animal looks something like a spider. Big ones with a legspread of 15 to 20 centimeters occur at great depths; smaller ones about 5 centimeters across may be found inshore.

The **horseshoe crab,** *Limulus polyphemus,* is an arachnid. Although sometimes referred to as the king crab, which is confusing, it has no relationship
or resemblance whatsoever to the king crab of Alaska, which is a true crab.
Limulus is a conspicuous animal of three sections: a rounded horseshoe-
shaped cephalothorax (head and chest area); an abdomen attached behind;
and a long, slim, triangular tail or telson that is quite rigid. The shell or
carapace of this animal is leathery, and has a chitinous texture like that of
toenails. The gills are located on the underside in the back part of the animal,
on the inside of a series of overlapping platelike appendages, which are called
book gills because they are like the pages of a book. There are 5 pairs of legs
with long pincer-like claws. The sixth pair located nearest the tail has no claws,
but ends in a ring of narrow elongated plates which may be extended and
fanned out. They are used by the animal to push its way through sand or
mud like a bulldozer. The tail is used to turn itself over if it is washed upside
down on the beach by the waves.

The horseshoe crab is generally seen only in the spring or early summer
when the females come in to sandy beaches to lay their eggs. They are
followed by 1 or 2, sometimes a train of smaller males. This parade comes
up onto the beach and the female lays her eggs in the sand right at the high,

Horseshoe crab, *Limulus polyphemus*

high-tide mark. The males fertilize the eggs, and all the horseshoe crabs go back to the sea. At the next high, high tide (about a month later), the sea comes up to the same spot, loosens the sand grains, and the newly hatched little horseshoe crabs scuttle down to the water. The mortality rate is very high, (but this species has persevered since the Paleozoic times, 600 millions of years ago). Later on, during the summer and fall, empty shells of *Limulus* are found all around Cape Ann. These are the cast skins of the animal. As with all arthropods, the crab must shed its skin to grow and these sheds or casts are quite common. The living creatures stay in the muddy sand and feed on small mollusks, worms, and crustaceans. The horseshoe crab is a real menace to the soft-shell clam industry, especially to newly seeded flats. *Limulus polyphemus* inhabits the entire eastern Atlantic from Maine to Mexico.

One insect is very common in the tide pools of Cape Ann. The **tide pool insect**, *Anurida maritima*, is a blue-black, steely-gray wingless animal not more than 1/2 centimeter in length. It is commonly found in large numbers clustering on the surface film of the water of lower tide pools on the rocky shore. A very primitive insect, a member of the order Collembola, this animal has a thick coating of hair, which collects enough air for it to breathe, in the form of bubbles, even if it is submerged for several days. *Anurida* lives in the intertidal area and is a scavenger that combs the rocks at low tide and consumes any suitable decaying detritus.

Anurida maritima

Mollusks — phylum Mollusca
(chitons, snails, bivalves, tusk shells, squid and octopi)

The phylum Mollusca is a large and important one. In spite of the great differences in appearance in these animals, like all members of a single phylum they have much in common. They all have soft bodies which at some stage of their development are encased in a shell. Their bodies consist of a head (not always clearly defined), a muscular foot, and a non-muscular visceral mass covered by a modified skin called a mantle.

The mantle secretes the shell which may be of many shapes and colors. It may completely surround the animal as in snails, bivalves and tusk shells; or occur in plates arranged dorsally, as in the chitons; or hidden inside, as in the squids and octopi; or found only in the embryonic form, as in the nudibranchs or sea slugs. Special muscles attach the body of a mollusk to its shell. The shell itself is usually made of calcium carbonate, limestone, and is often laid down in three layers. The outer layer is a horny skin-like material, the periostracum. The middle layer is the main portion of the shell and is made of large crystals of calcium carbonate. The inner layer contains thin plates that overlap like shingles. When light is reflected from these plates, one gets a pearly effect. This inner layer is called nacre or mother-of-pearl. As the animal grows, the main growth is at the edge of the shell and is formed by the mantle.

The mouth of a mollusk is always at its anterior end. It is the opening or entrance to the digestive tract. In the chitons and bivalves, it is nothing more than that, but in the higher mollusks, we find the development of a head with a mouth or buccal cavity, and an increase of sense organs. In all mollusks except the bivalves, the mouth leads into the buccal cavity which contains a radula or tongue-like structure peculiar to mollusks. This radula is ribbon-like, covered with rows of sharp tiny teeth arranged in transverse patterns. Different in each species, it is used to obtain food by scraping algae off rocks or boring holes in other mollusks.

The foot of a mollusk is used for locomotion and usually lies on the ventral side. It differs in the squids and octopi, where it surrounds the mouth and forms the so-called arms or tentacles of these animals. The chitons have a broad, fleshy foot with which they cling tightly to rocks or other substrates. Bivalves and tusk shells have a highly extendible and contractile foot for digging in sand. The snails have a strong muscular foot for locomotion which often has a horny operculum attached. This is a toenail-like device that effectively seals the aperture of a snail when the animal has withdrawn into the shell.

Mollusks are one of the groups of animals whose history is well-known. Fossil specimens have been found right back to Cambrian times — 600 million years ago. Even the earliest mollusks are so highly organized that it is believed that they had existed for a long time before the first fossils were formed. Shells of fossil mollusks have helped to correlate many rock formations. Economically, mollusks are important for dating oil and other mineral-bearing rocks. Living mollusks are important food items for man. All classes of mollusks are found on the western Atlantic seaboard, but not all are common on Cape Ann.

Chitons, class Amphineura, are the most primitive of the mollusks that are common. They are small oval animals with a firm, fleshy foot below, topped by a series of 8 overlapping shells or plates. The protruding upper part of the foot immediately under the shells is called the girdle, and may or may not have spines. The overlapping shells are joined in such a way that the animal can curl like an armadillo and also adapt itself to the contour of the rock or other place of attachment. This adaptation and the fact that the foot acts like a suction cup permits chitons to adhere very tightly to any rock surface. They can hang on even when swept by the most powerful surf. The chitons of Cape Ann are usually small. One species may be found, but it is uncommon.

Chiton, *Ischnochiton ruber,* is a light-red animal with yellowish mottlings, smooth plates, and a granulated girdle. It can reach a length of 2 centimeters, but it is usually much smaller. Found on exposed rocks in the Kelp Zone, it usually occurs on the bottom of deep tide pools, but may be found on the rocks in the Irish Moss Zone.

Snails, class Gastropoda, the stomach-footed animals, have several peculiarities that make them different from other mollusks. One peculiarity occurs during the larval period when a phenomenon called torsion occurs. Suddenly the animal, which up to now has been bilaterally symmetrical, grows with a twist of $180°$, so that the forward part of the body moves to the right and the anus is brought around to the front above the mouth. The animal then grows in a coiled manner to result in the typical snail shell. There is a further refinement to this torsion in the sub-class which includes animals without shells — the sea slugs (nudibranchs) and the sea butterflies (pteropods). These animals become untwisted when they reach adult life. Though they look symmetrical on the outside, they are not. They

Chiton, *Ischnochiton ruber*

have a single kidney and gill, and the genital pore and anus off-center on one side.

The **tortoise-shell limpet** or Chinaman's hat, *Acmaea testudinalis,* is very common on Cape Ann. Almost every tide pool below the Barnacle Zone contains one or more limpets. They have conical shells of a tortoise-shell color and look just like a coolie's hat. The low spire and broad round shape give nothing for the waves to catch onto; so, with the foot acting like a suction cup, they can occupy the most exposed portion on the rocks with safety. The large fleshy foot is at the bottom of the shell. There is no operculum.

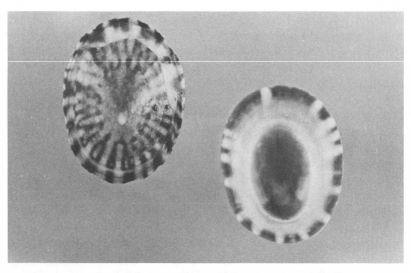

Tortoise-shell limpet or Chinaman's hat, *Acmaea testudinalis*

A limpet can move about on its foot as well as stick tightly to a desired spot. The buccal cavity contains a very long radula (tongue) with which it rasps off the algae it eats. The tortoise-shell limpet browses in a limited range in its particular tide pool or rocky area, and generally goes back to a certain spot to rest after eating. On softer rocks than Cape Ann granite this homing or resting spot can actually be indented.

Periwinkles are true snails or gastropods with coiled shells. They live on rocks from the splash area all through the intertidal area, and are herbivorous. Four species are commonly found on Cape Ann.

Lacuna vincta is an abundant **periwinkle** that lives on rocks and algae from the Arctic to Rhode Island. It is small, 7 millimeters in size. The shell is delicate, a yellowish-brown in color, and covered with a thin periostracum. It has a very open rounded aperture and three abrupt, strongly indented but rounded body whorls. The apex of the shell is purplish. One needs a hand lens to study this animal. It is found on rocks, algae, and eelgrass in the intertidal area all around Cape Ann, except on the exposed seashores.

Periwinkle, *Lacuna vincta*

The **common periwinkle**, *Littorina littorea*, is one of the most conspicuous animals that is always present on the rocks of Cape Ann. Like the barnacle, it has a zone named after it. These round, low-spired stout shells measure about 2 centimeters in every direction. They live in great quantities all over the rocks, on and under rockweed and Irish moss. They also live in tide pools and on rocks that plunge down into the Kelp Zone. The common periwinkle is usually very dark gray, but may be brownish and sometimes have bands which show up more when the shell is wet. The opening of the shell is a slightly

Left to right: Common periwinkle, *Littorina littorea,*
smooth periwinkle, *Littorina obtusata* and rough periwinkle, *Littorina saxatilis*

compressed O. The outer lip is quite thick, but narrows to a sharp edge and is lined with black. The base of the columella (the column that the shell twists around) is white, and continues part of the way up the edge of the aperture. A horny, dark-brown operculum is present, which effectively seals the animal from drying out when it is withdrawn into its shell. The buccal cavity contains a radula (tongue) with which it scrapes algae off the rocks or seaweed as it moves along. Originally European, the common periwinkle has spread across and around the northern Atlantic, moving southward from Canada. It now ranges as far south as New Jersey.

The smooth or **little green periwinkle,** *Littorina obtusata,* is a small snail with a stout well-rounded body whorl and a smooth shiny shell. It may be green or distinctly yellow. It lives in the mid-tide area in the Rockweed Zone, where it is indistinguishable from rockweed in color, or in tide pools and on wet rocks. Generally smaller than the common periwinkle and larger than the rough, it grazes on intertidal algae and ranges from Labrador to Cape Hatteras.

The **rough periwinkle,** *Littorina saxatilis,* is similar to but smaller than the common periwinkle. It is a light yellowish-gray in color, and has more prominently indented whorls on its shell. It ranges up to 1½ centimeters in size, and lives in the upper limits of the intertidal zones between the Black Zone and the Barnacle Zone. The inside edge of the lip of the rough periwinkle is light but the aperture is dark brown. There is no white area at the base of the columella. The operculum is a dark yellow and forms such an effective plug that the rough periwinkle can live out of water for a month. It ranges from the Arctic seas to New Jersey.

The slipper shell or **boat shell,** *Crepidula fornicata,* grows up to 5 centimeters in length, and is found occasionally in sheltered rocky pools or attached to other mollusks. It has a dusky-white oval shell which enables one slipper shell limpet to fasten itself tightly to the shell of another. Often three or more are found stacked together like a tower. The underside of the shell is open and half-decked with a smooth portion that originates at the small or anterior end. Although not as common as the tortoise-shell limpet in the Cape Ann area, the slipper shell occurs from Prince Edward Island south to Texas, and is much more numerous in the South.

Slipper shell or boat shell, *Crepidula fornicata*

The sand-collar snail or **Atlantic moon snail,** *Polinices duplicatus,* is the uncommon more southerly species that is found from Massachusetts Bay to North Carolina. It differs from the northern moon snail in having a hard, round, brownish callus covering the umbilicus. It is found in the Annisquam River.

The common **northern moon snail,** *Lunatia heros,* is a large round bluewhite snail with a small and very deep umbilicus (hole around which the whorls coil) and a large slightly triangular aperture that is brownish inside. The animal itself is grayish and seems too big for its shell, but can pull itself

Moon snails, left top and bottom, *Lunatia heros*
right top and bottom, *Polinices duplicatus* with callus

inside and shut its aperture with a large dark brown horny operculum. It is
often found on beaches in the sand long after animal and snail have disappeared.
Hold this brown operculum up to the light and see how delicately it is marked.
The moon snail lives in sand and mud, where it plows along in the subtidal
area looking for clams on which it feeds, engulfing the clam with its foot, and
drilling into it with its toothed tongue or radula. It ranges from the Gulf of St.
Lawrence to North Carolina to Texas and is very common on all sandy, muddy
areas of Cape Ann, especially in Ipswich Bay. The egg case of the moon snail is
often found in the early summer on sheltered beaches and in shallow water
in the form of a sand collar.

The **dog whelk,** *Thais lapillus,* is a species of snail which occurs abundantly
on the rocky intertidal area of Cape Ann. Found at all seasons, the snails are
generally white. The younger shells are a glistening china-white with a pointed
spire and an elongated white-lined aperture. The older the shell, the thicker it
becomes and the color turns off-white. Some dog whelks are yellow, orange
or brown and sometimes banded with white. The radula of this species is

Dog whelk, *Thais lapillus*

adapted to boring and a dog whelk can easily bore a hole through the shell of
a blue mussel or a thicker-shelled mollusk and eat the animal inside. They
also feed on barnacles. The anal gland of a dog whelk contains a minute
quantity of purple dye which may be seen if the shell is crushed and the tiny
green gland spread on a white tissue, or on your fingers, and left in full sunlight. The smear will turn purple. This gland was used like that of the murex
shell of the Mediterranean to make the Tyrian purple dye famous in classical
times.

Dog whelk eggs can be found in the late spring and early summer on Cape
Ann. They are laid in crevices in the rock or at the base of the seaweed in the
Rockweed Zone. Resembling tiny grains of rice, or vases, the egg cases are
attached to the rock at one end. Each egg case contains up to 100 eggs, and a
female dog whelk may lay as many as 200 egg cases. The eggs develop in the
case right through the larval stages and the tiny-shelled dog whelks emerge and
move quickly down the intertidal area to live.

True whelks belong to the family Buccinidae, and are large heavy pear-
shaped snails with an aperture notched anteriorly to form a short wide canal.
They are carnivorous inhabitants of northern seas. One species may be found
off Cape Ann.

The **waved whelk** or common northern whelk, *Buccinum undatum,* occasionally occurs in deep tide pools off Cape Ann, but is always present offshore; farther north along the Maine coast it is more common inshore. A large (up to 10 centimeters long), tan to pinkish snail with a prominent spire, it has longitudinal ridges running from the aperture to the spire, undulating slightly as they cross the whorls of the shell. The shell is quite thick and often unevenly textured where a layer of calcite has been damaged and replaced. The body of this snail is spotted with black like a Dalmatian dog. It is a handsome lively carnivorous creature, often a nuisance to lobster fishermen because it is attracted to the bait in their traps. It is an edible species eaten extensively in Europe, but rarely in the United States.

Egg cases of the waved whelk are often washed up on the shore. They form a mass about the size of a baseball of pearly-colored, oval egg cases, each as large as a little fingernail, containing hundreds of eggs. The individual egg cases are clustered together, overlapping each other like shingles. Old-time sailors used these egg cases instead of soap. They are known as merman's soap.

The **Stimpson's colus,** *Colus stimpsoni,* has a large cylindrical shell, 12 centimeters long with an oval aperture almost half the length of the shell. It

Waved whelk, *Buccinum undatum*

Stimpson's colus, *Colus stimpsoni*

has smooth strong whorls with very fine spiral lines. The shell is chalky white with a brown skin or periostracum. It is common in sand in shallow subtidal areas from the Gulf of St. Lawrence to North Carolina and may be found in Ipswich Bay.

The **ten-ridged whelk** or New England neptune, *Neptunea decemcostata*, is a 10-centimeter snail that is grayish-white, with 7 to 10 very heavy spiral cords on the body whorl and an irregular oval aperture that is white inside. It

Ten-ridged whelk, *Neptunea decemcostata*

lays a cylindrical tower-like egg mass. From Nova Scotia to Massachusetts it is common in two to three meters of water on sandy bottoms, often off rocky shores, and occurs in Ipswich Bay.

The **New England nassa,** *Nassarius trivittatus,* is a small (up to 2 centimeters long), gray carnivorous snail with a pyramidal shape strongly segmented with definite body whorls that are neatly beaded. The aperture is somewhat oval with a sharp strong brownish-colored outer lip. The operculum is ragged-edged to fit the uneven aperture. The animals live on clean sand and will congregate in great numbers around and on a piece of dead fish. They are very active, moving around on a light-colored foot peppered with tiny dark spots. It has fleshy protuberances or cirri on its tail or caudal end. Present on sandy beaches from Nova Scotia to Georgia, it appears all around Cape Ann. The dead shells are favorites for tiny hermit crabs.

The **Eastern mud nassa,** *Nassarius obsoletus,* occurs in large numbers on all the Cape Ann mud flats. It is a smoothly whorled, peanut-shaped snail with a large oval aperture and a strong heavy lip, dark brown outside and in, and the shell is often eroded. The body is a deep gray, faintly spotted, with no cirri on the caudal end. This snail is active and moves along a mud flat leaving a definitive groove behind. The operculum is horny, blackish, and quite smooth. The egg capsules of this snail are often found on cord grass or eelgrass. They are transparent, angular, and very numerous. From Canada to northern Florida, this snail is abundant.

Sea butterflies or flying snails, pteropods, are deep-sea, pelagic gastropods which form part of the plankton population offshore. They are derived from typical gastropods, but there are several anatomical differences. Some have shells only in the embryonic stage; some have delicate glossy translucent shells. They have a rudimentary foot with a pair of wing-like flaps with which they swim. They occur in huge numbers out at sea in such large quantities that they are an important food for certain whales and oceanic fish. They swim down in the daylight and at night come up to the surface to feed. It is then that they may be caught by a storm and blown ashore. Infrequently, they have been found after a winter storm up on beaches and in tide pools on Cape Ann.

Clione sp. is a sea butterfly that has lost its shell and swims with two expansions of its foot, its wings. It has a conically-shaped body tapering to a fine point posteriorly and the wings are stubby affairs set well up towards the front of the animal. Between the wings is the buccal cavity lined with a ring of

New England nassa, *Nassarius trivittatus*

Eastern mud nassa, *Nassarius obsoletus*

Sea butterfly, *Clione* sp.

fleshy tentacles. The animal is transparent but has some color in the posterior half. It occurs in huge schools in the surface waters of colder oceans, and is eaten by baleen whales.

Sea slugs or nudibranchs are gastropods which entirely lack a shell in the adult stage. They have no true gill and breathe either through their skin or through the projections on the dorsal surface. Varying in size, shape and color, sea slugs are of two types: one, the oval dorids with gills on their backs and having one pair of tentacles and feeding on sponges and bryozoa; the other, the eolids, which have cerata (fleshy protuberances from the main body) and 2 pairs of tentacles. Nudibranchs are generally of an oval shape with a large foot underneath and a mouth containing a radula. They have many different shapes and numbers of the dorsal cerata. Some are tiny and a hand lens is necessary to examine them. They feed on hydroids and sea anemones. They are undisturbed by the stinging cells in the anemones and incorporate these cells into their own cerata for their defense. There are a good many species of sea slugs on the rocky shores of Cape Ann.

The **plumed sea slug**, *Aeolidia papillosa*, is the largest sea slug found on Cape Ann. It is often found in the fall and early winter in the tide pools of the

Plumed sea slug, *Aeolidia papillosa*

Irish Moss Zone or near the common sea anemone. Never numerous, this sea slug is an orange-beige color or a milk-chocolate brown and often matches the color of the sea anemones it feeds on. It is usually about 4 centimeters long, but can be twice that. It is covered with cerata which are bushy and tend to part like a mane.

The **salmon-gilled sea slug,** *Coryphella salmonacea,* is a large sea slug, never more than 3 centimeters long. It has an elongated body, tapering back to an acute point. The cerata are much longer in front than in back, and are a salmon-pink color tipped with white. They are evenly spaced from front to back. The tentacles are white, set above a squarish mouth. Look for them on hydroids and seaweeds.

Coryphella rufibranchialis is common, and shaped like an isosceles triangle. It has tufts of scarlet cerata arranged at regular intervals on the sides of the body. The tip of each tuft is white, in strong contrast to the red below. The head is much broader than the tail, and the whole animal is usually less than 3 centimeters long. It is found on hydroids, especially *Tubularia.*

The **bushy-backed slug,** *Dendronotus frondosus,* is a reddish-brown animal usually less than 1½ centimeters. It is dark on the dorsal surface with light-colored, almost translucent cerata that are numerously branched like a tree or certain seaweeds.

Sea slug, *Coryphella rufibranchialis*

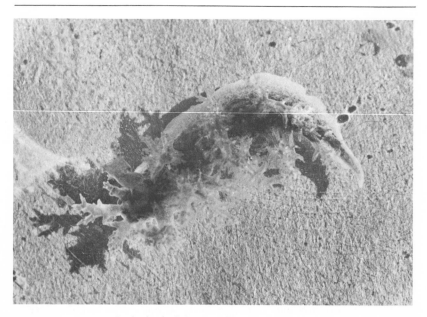

Bushy-backed slug, *Dendronotus frondosus*

Onchidoris aspera is a small white or cream-colored sea slug. Less than 1 centimeter in length, it has an elongated body rounded on both ends with a pair of tentacles anteriorly, and a star-shaped gill posteriorly near the anus. The back or dorsal surface is covered with tubercles of varying size. It is found at low tide near the low-water mark feeding on barnacles from easternmost Maine to Newport, Rhode Island.

Onchidoris fusca is a large dull yellowish-white sea slug with a roseate tone. This is due to the coloring of the bluntly rounded papillae with which the back is covered. Each papilla or tubercle is tipped with reddish-brown while their bases are yellow. The gill is shaped like a radiating star and the branching parts are yellow surrounded by a dark brown area. The tentacles are pinkish to white. *O. fusca* moves fairly rapidly and is an active sea slug, busily searching out colonies of bryozoa on which to feed. It is found in the lowest intertidal area under rocks, from Boston north.

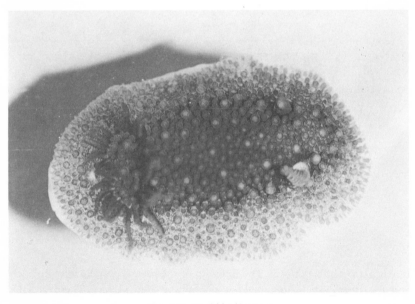

Sea slug, *Onchidoris aspera*

The **common marsh snail**, *Melampus bidentatus*, has a horn-colored shell about 1 centimeter long with a short conical spire. It is oval, and the broadest point is about two-thirds of the way towards the top of the shell. The aper-

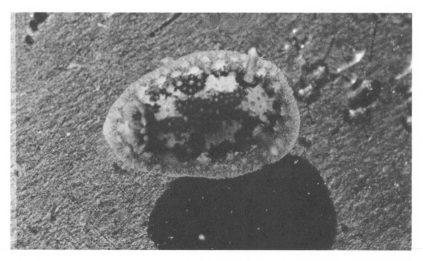

Onchidoris fusca

Common marsh snail, *Melampus bidentatus*

ture is narrow and also oval. The inner lip of the shell is covered with enamel and has 2 teeth. The whole shell has a definitely shiny surface. These are salt-water pulmonate snails; that is, they have a lung cavity and breathe air. Their eyes are on the ends of the tentacles. Although they live in salt marshes from Prince Edward Island to the Gulf of Mexico, they are not strictly marine animals. They are usually found in the upper marsh climbing on the grasses to keep out of the salt water.

Clams, mussels, oysters, etc., are in the class Pelecypoda, the hatchet-footed animals. Pelecypods are two-shelled animals, bivalves, whose entire bodies except the siphon and the foot are contained inside the shells. The mantle, a soft flap of skin, encloses the body mass except at the opening between the shells. Food and water are brought into the mouth and gills by the siphon, which consists of two tubes, sometimes enclosed in one large tube, one of which brings a stream of water into and around the animal. The other tube expels the water minus food and oxygen, and carries waste products. The 2 shells on the valves are kept together by a strong muscle. This muscle is what we eat in the scallop. Sometimes there are 2 muscles. There is a kind of hinge arrangement at the top of these shells. The point of attachment of the muscle or muscles of a bivalve may be seen on the inside of the shell in the form of a large scar.

The mantle secretes the shell, which grows as the animal does. Growth lines may be seen on the outside of the shells. Some pelecypods, like the mussels, possess a device for anchoring them to the substrate, called byssal threads. These threads may be 3 centimeters long and are spun from a gland in the foot and placed in a fan-like network on the substrate. Many of the bivalves found on rocky coasts have byssal threads, otherwise they would be swept away by the waves. Most pelecypods are found in sand and mud, but some also occur on the rocky shores of Cape Ann.

The **common awning clam,** *Solemya velum,* has a small, dark-brown, fragile shell usually from 3 to 5 centimeters in size. The oval valves (shells of a bivalve) are of equal size, gaping posteriorly and anteriorly. The shell is covered by a thick membrane or skin-like periostracum which extends beyond the shell in a coarse square-cut fringe. Usually buried in sand, *Solemya* does not swim actively. Often found on beaches after a storm, it ranges from Nova Scotia to Florida and is found in the Annisquam River and Little River regions of Cape Ann.

The **file yoldia,** *Yoldia limatula* is a very compressed thin, 6-centimeter shell, greenish tan-brown outside, whitish inside. It is elliptical and gapes at both ends; and the hinge has a row of interlocking teeth on each side. Living in sand beyond low water, it is common from Maine to New Jersey and is sometimes cast up on the beaches of Gloucester Harbor and Ipswich Bay.

The **blue mussel,** *Mytilus edulis,* is the common edible mussel. It grows in huge numbers on rocks and in tide pools from the Barnacle Zone to the Irish Moss Zone around Cape Ann, and may be found in all sizes from tiny seed mussels up to 10 centimeters in length, at all seasons of the year. Locally, patches of mussels come and go. A tide pool and surrounding rocks will be

Common awning clam, *Solemya velum*

File yoldia, *Yoldia limatula*

full of mussels for a few years, and suddenly there will be no large ones, but only a scattering of seed mussels. Winter ice can clean out a mussel bed for a season, but these animals are so prolific that they soon build up another population. The blue mussel is pear-shaped with byssal threads forming at the

Blue mussel, *Mytilus edulis*

narrow end. They vary from violet-blue to a soft chalky blue and have a dark-brownish horny epidermis that soon sloughs off dead and broken shells. Inside they are lined with a bluish mother-of-pearl, nacre, that is quite beautiful. Blue mussels are edible and have a very delicate flavor. However, care should be taken to eat mussels that live in an area completely free of any contamination such as sewer outlets or polluted surface runoffs. All bivalves are filter feeders and can concentrate in their intestinal tracts bacteria and other substances harmful to man, but harmless to themselves.

The **ribbed mussel**, *Modiolus demissus,* is found half imbedded in the mud of the steep marsh banks and in among the roots of the cord grass, *Spartina alterniflora.* It closely resembles the blue mussel, *Mytilus edulis* of the rocky shores, except that it is strongly marked on the outside of the shell with radiating ribs which are deeply indented near the hinges, and less so on the broader anterior part. The shell is brittle and has a finely scalloped edge. The color is greenish rather than blue. It is up to 10 centimeters in length and ranges south to Georgia from Prince Edward Island. These mussels tend to grow in clumps and must live in the mid-tidal part of the marsh. When they are feeding, the ribbed mussels tend to ingest a good deal of inedible material as they filter water through their digestive system. They get

Ribbed mussel, *Modiolus demissus*

rid of this debris in pseudofeces made up of mucus, mud and indigestible particles. This matter tends to pile up around the shells unless there are very strong currents, and ultimately the mussels would bury themselves if they did not move up. The hummocky appearance of the marsh is due to clumps of ribbed mussels at the mid-tide level.

The **horse mussel,** *Modiolus modiolus,* is a larger mussel than the blue, and found deeper down the tide line, from the Irish Moss Zone into the Kelp Zone. The shell is heavy and wedge-shaped, from 10 to 15 centimeters in length. It has a dark brown outer skin that ends in a characteristic yellowish outer fringe at the wide end of the shell. Inside, the shell lining is a pink pearly lustre and occasionally pearls are present inside the shell. The horse mussel has many heavy byssal threads that anchor it securely in the most exposed locations, in the crevices of open tide pools, and in mud and gravel between rocks from shallow water down to 130 meters or more. The byssal threads are so entangled that debris, sand, bits of shells, seaweed, etc. are caught in them, and a specialized environment is formed where one can find certain animals such as worms and brittle stars and other mollusks.

The thorny or **spiny jingle shell,** *Anomia aculeata,* is a small, 1-centimeter, thin, translucent yellowish shell that has unequal valves. The left or upper valve is the larger, and is dome-shaped. Its surface is roughened by prickly scales. The lower valve is very thin, concave, and has a round hole just below the hinge through which the byssal threads pass and attach the jingle to the substrate which may be a rock or another shell. The jingle is

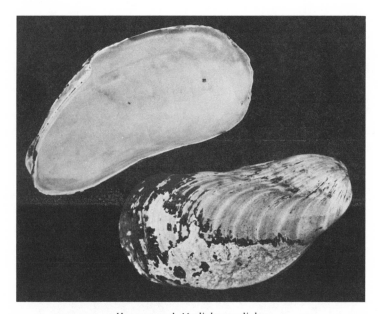

Horse mussel, *Modiolus modiolus*

Spiny jingle shell, *Anomia aculeata*

fastened very tightly. They range from Labrador to North Carolina and are found on stones in the Ipswich Bay, Annisquam River, and Gloucester Harbor area of Cape Ann.

The **waved astarte**, *Astarte undata*, is a strong heavy brownish shell about 3 centimeters across, approximately triangular, with about 10 heavy concentric ridges. The beaks curve inwards. This shell has a reddish-brown periostracum, but is gleaming white inside, and lives in mud from Canada to Massachusetts below low-water mark. In Ipswich Bay and Gloucester Harbor it is uncommon.

Waved astarte, *Astarte undata*

The ocean quahog, black or **mahogany clam**, *Arctica islandica*, has a strong heavy shell, almost round, with a thick dark-brown to black periostracum. This is an edible species that lives in sub-tidal sand from Newfoundland to North Carolina. Common in Ipswich Bay, the shells are found on adjacent beaches of Cape Ann.

The northern quahog or **hard-shell clam**, *Mercenaria mercenaria*, is a heavy thick clam. It is almost round, of a pinkish-brown color, and the outside of its shell is covered with concentric growth lines. Inside, the shell is a porcelain-white, often with a blue or purple stain. This is the shell the Indians used for wampum. They made beads of it and strung them. The purple parts were considered more valuable than the white. Quahogs are easily identified

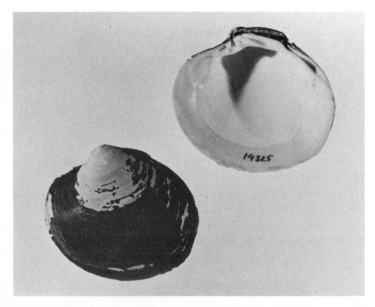

Mahogany clam, *Arctica islandica*

Hard-shell clam, *Mercenaria mercenaria*

because they have a heart-shaped depression, the lunule, just below the beak of the shell. This is seen when both valves are closed and the shell is held sideways with the beak towards you. This is an important clam commercially south of Boston, where it is dug in quantity and sold, depending upon size, under the names of quahog or hard-shell clam, little neck or cherrystone. The cherrystone is the smallest and the least mature quahog. They range from the Gulf of St. Lawrence to Florida. Occasionally they are found in sand and mud around Cape Ann, but are not numerous enough to be dug commercially in this area.

The **amethystine gem shell,** *Gemma gemma,* is a pea-sized tannish-purple shell, one of the Venus clams. It is quite round and is shiny white inside. It lives in huge quantities in sheltered sandy places and may be so numerous that the larvae of the soft-shell clam, *Mya arenaria,* cannot find a place to settle. They are often found broken on the drift line of sheltered sandy beaches of Cape Ann. It ranges from Nova Scotia to Texas.

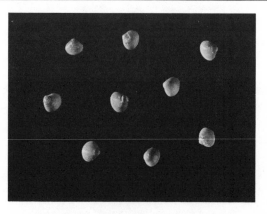

Amethystine gem shell, *Gemma gemma*

The **false angel wing,** *Petricola pholadiformis,* has an oval chalky-white, elongated, stoutly-ribbed shell. Single valves are often found in the inter-tidal area in heavy sand. A Caribbean subspecies is a rock borer, boring into clay and soft rocks. But on Cape Ann, where it cannot penetrate the ever-present granite, it lives in peat, mud, and heavy sand. It is closely associated with the soft-shell clam, *Mya arenaria.* Its range is from eastern Canada to the Gulf of Mexico and is common on intertidal sand all around Cape Ann.

The **northern dwarf tellin,** *Tellina agilis,* has small, (1-centimeter), fragile, rose or coffee-colored shells of elliptical shape. They are glossy and iridescent,

False angel wing, *Petricola pholadiformis*

Northern dwarf tellin, *Tellina agilis*

occasionally with prominent growth lines. They live in sandy mud in the inter-tidal area and are common from Canada to Georgia. The empty shells are often found on the drift or strand line of the Gloucester Harbor, Annisquam River areas of Cape Ann.

The duck clam, **baltic macoma**, *Macoma balthica*, has a small white or pinkish shell, less than 2½ centimeters in length with a pale thin, flaky peri-ostracum. The shell is somewhat squatly triangular in shape and is variable in

Baltic macoma, *Macoma balthica*

color and thickness. The shell is thin and pure white, pink or yellow when living on sandy bottoms, but thicker and dusky red or blue in muddy areas. It lives from the Arctic to Georgia, and is common all around Cape Ann.

The **razor clam**, merman's razor, Atlantic jacknife clam, *Ensis directus*, is the common razor clam of the Atlantic coast from Labrador south. It has a long, narrow shell of 15 to 17 centimeters, slightly curved with open rounded ends. The shell is covered with a thin brownish periostracum, and is often found cast up on a mud-sand beach. It lives along sandy bottoms at about low-water mark, standing vertically with its posterior end up and siphons extended into the water. At the slightest vibration of the sand flat caused by a footstep or boat grounding, they dig rapidly out of sight. They can dig faster than a man with a clam rake, and so are not often dug commercially, although they make excellent eating. They live in Ipswich Bay and the Annisquam and Little Rivers of Cape Ann.

The **ribbed pod shell**, *Siliqua costata*, is a fragile, thin shell of oval shape. It has a shiny greenish periostracum over a white shell. Inside, the shell is purplish with a strong rib extending down from the hinge. It lives in sand in intertidal areas from the Gulf of St. Lawrence to North Carolina and is often found cast up on both sheltered and open beaches, such as those of Ipswich Bay and the Annisquam River.

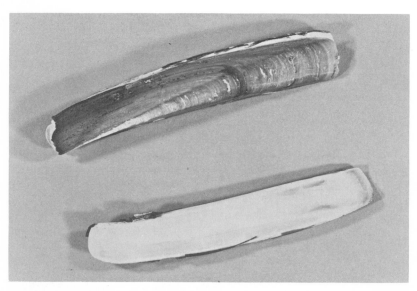

Razor clam, *Ensis directus*

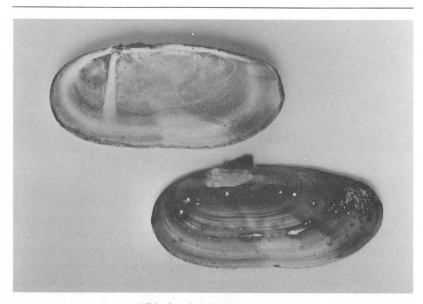

Ribbed pod shell, *Siliqua costata*

The **surf clam**, hen clam, *Spisula solidissima,* is the largest bivalve on the Atlantic coast. It may be up to 18 centimeters long and has a thick, heavy, chalky-white shell covered with a thin periostracum. It lives in sand just below the low-water mark out to the 30-meter mark. As its name implies, it can survive in unprotected areas as well as sheltered ones. Noted for good eating, it is gathered at extra low tides by wading offshore and probing the sand with bare feet or a pitchfork. From Nova Scotia to South Carolina and all around Cape Ann it is common.

Surf clam or hen clam, *Spisula solidissima*

The **soft-shell clam**, Ipswich clam, steamer clam, *Mya arenaria,* is one of the most valuable shellfish of the Cape Ann region and is much in demand for clambakes and seafood dinners. Not eaten raw like the quahog of Cape Cod, it is fried, or steamed in the shell and eaten by grasping the animal by its neck, actually its siphon, and dipping it in clam broth and/or butter, then popping the entire animal into one's mouth. The shell is chalky white-gray with elliptical valves which are unequal. They gape at both ends and the left valve has a spoon-shaped tooth at the hinge line which fits into a corresponding hole in the right valve. These clams live buried in mud or sand when the tide

Soft-shell clam or steamer clam, *Mya arenaria*

is out. When the tide comes in and covers the clam flats, the animal extends its siphon through the mud or sand into the water and feeds by filtering food from the water which it pumps through itself. There are 2 tubes in the siphon, one for intake, and the other for expelling water. When the clam flat, exposed at low tide, is vibrated, these clams react to danger by a sudden digging of themselves deeper into the mud. This produces a squirt of water from the siphon and is an immediate indication of where to dig. Clams may not be taken in Massachusetts without a permit or license that is granted by each coastal town. Many clam flats are closed because they are polluted by red tide, sewage or other runoff from the land, and no clams should be eaten unless one knows that they come from an open, uncontaminated flat. The range is from Labrador to North Carolina, including Gloucester Harbor, Annisquam and Little Rivers, and Ipswich Bay.

The **red-nosed clam,** Atlantic rock borer, *Hiatella arctica,* is found in the lower tide pools on the rocks of Cape Ann. It is often associated with the horse mussel, and may be recognized by the bright red siphons, which may be seen poking up among the byssal threads. Generally small in size, locally it may be as large as 5 centimeters. It has a square chalky-white shell with a yellowish epidermis. The 2 valves do not fit together tightly. There is a large gap at the posterior end through which emerges the stout siphon. This rock borer forms a very strong set of byssal threads, which when attached and entangled with those of the horse mussel, firmly anchors it in extremely exposed situations. In places where the rocks are softer than Cape Ann granite, such as limestone, soft sandstone, clay or cement, *Hiatella* actually bores into the rock. There it settles permanently. It can make a hole as deep as 20 centimeters. Great damage may be done to concrete seawalls and break-waters by these mollusks. *Hiatella* ranges from Greenland south, and is especially abundant in northern waters.

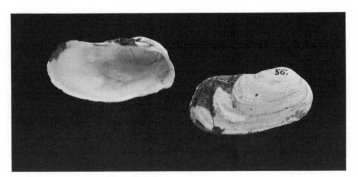

Red-nosed clam, *Hiatella arctica*

The **Arctic wedge clam,** *Mesodesma arctatum,* is a small sturdy ovate clam, 5 centimeters or less in length, which may be found in quantity on the sandy beaches of Ipswich Bay. The shells are quite thick and are covered on the outside with a thin pale-brown periostracum or skin which flakes off after the animal dies and the shell has been exposed to sun and weather on a beach. The growth lines are prominent. Inside they are a shiny china-white and the palial line is very definite. At the hinge there is a spoon-shaped cavity where the cartilaginous ligament attaches. One valve, or shell, has steep prominent teeth and the other deep grooves in which the teeth fit. This is a common species and sometimes there are so many cast up on the beaches that they form white windrows on the sands. *Mesodesma* is found from Virginia to eastern Canada.

The **great piddock,** *Zirfaea crispata,* is a conspicuous shell that is occasionally found washed up on the beach, on the sandy or muddy beaches of Cape Ann, especially in the Ipswich Bay areas. It is a boring clam that digs itself into mud, clay or even soft rocks and may live from the intertidal zone to a depth of 100 meters. The proportion of this shell is stout and the 2 valves touch each other only at the hinge line and at one other place opposite this. The shells are whitish and each has 2 distinct areas that are separated by a diagonal line slanting back towards the siphon. The anterior part of the shell is rough and the growth lines are made up of raised scales. The posterior part is smoother but has distinct growth lines. Each valve of this animal is somewhat twisted. It is fairly common from eastern Canada to New Jersey.

The **Gould's Pandora,** *Pandora gouldiana,* is a thin chalky-white bivalve whose shell is often worn down to the mother-of-pearl underlayers. Roughly oblong, and about 3 centimeters long, this shell is smoothly angular outside,

Arctic wedge clam, *Mesodesma arctatum*

Great piddock, *Zirfaea crispata*

with a ridge running obliquely down from the hinge and another ridge almost parallel to the upper edge. The inside of the shell is strongly marked. One shell is toothed; the other is grooved to fit the teeth. A common shell from Quebec to New Jersey, it lives in sand near rocky areas, and is found in Gloucester Harbor cast up on the harbor beaches.

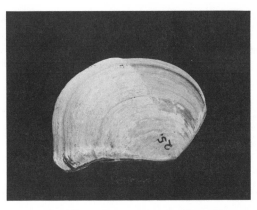

Gould's Pandora, *Pandora gouldiana*

Starfish, brittle stars, sea urchins and sea cucumbers — phylum Echinodermata (spiny-skinned animals)

The echinoderms are an important phylum in the intertidal regions. All subdivisions in the phylum have 3 things in common: a spiny skin or a modification thereof; a 5-part radial symmetry; and an internal water-vascular system.

The spiny skin is the result of lime or calcareous plates embedded in the skin, with spines projecting to the outside. In the starfish and brittle stars these plates articulate with each other so that the animal can bend easily; the projecting spines are short.

In the rigid sea urchins, the spines can be long, and serve both for protection and locomotion. The sea cucumbers also have calcareous plates of various shapes embedded throughout a thick leathery skin. These have no articulation and no spines.

All groups of echinoderms have 5-part radial symmetry. The starfish and brittle stars have 5 arms. Bend these arms down, curl them around, fill in the space between, and there is a resemblance to a sea urchin. Sea cucumbers, although they tend to look like old sacks, have, when viewed from the head end, a radial arrangement of parts based on 5-part symmetry. All echinoderms, however, have bilateral symmetry in the larval stages.

The water-vascular system common to all echinoderms is unique to this phylum. It consists of a radial canal that surrounds the mouth from which 5 canals branch off, one for each of the 5 arms, or derivatives. These arms have a large number of tube feet, which are extendible little tubes that in many cases end in a suction cup. The whole system is connected to the outside by the stone canal that runs from the ring canal to the madreporite or round sieve plate on the outer skin. It is through the madreporite that salt-water is drawn into the water-vascular system, and the hydraulic pressure raised or lowered. The muscular system can move itself by these or by using the suction cups and can attach itself firmly to a rock or some other firm surface.

The cavity of the water-vascular system is part of the coelom. It is this possession of the coelom that relates the echinoderms with the phyla from which the protochordates and finally the chordates are developed.

Echinoderms can move in any direction, and the nerve ganglia are not con-centrated in the head region, as they are in a bilaterally symmetrical animal. They are found all over, on the tips of the arms on starfish and brittle stars, and on the entire skin in the others.

The sea stars, Asteroidea, (star-shaped animals) are numerous in deep water off Cape Ann, but only three species are commonly found in the intertidal area.

The **blood sea star,** *Henricia sanguinolenta,* is a brilliant red animal from 10 to 15 centimeters in diameter. It has smooth skin with very long slender arms that often curl up at the tips. The underside is a light yellow color. There

Blood sea star, *Henricia sanguinolenta*

is a small disc on top and one groove on the ventral side with the tube feet in 2 rows along the ambulacral groove. It can be found in deep tide pools, usually in the darkest regions on all the rocky shores of Cape Ann.

The **common starfish**, *Asterias forbesi*, is a common animal on the rocky shores of Cape Ann. Its range is from Maine to the Gulf of Mexico, but it is rarely found north of Massachusetts. It is found in tide pools, clinging to rocks, under seaweed and in crevices of sea walls and rocks. This is a conspicuous animal, about 15 centimeters in diameter. It may be as large as 30

Common starfish, *Asterias forbesi*

centimeters in diameter, and have 4, 6, or 7 arms, but those commonly found on Cape Ann usually have 5 arms. Arms torn off are quickly regenerated. The skin of the dorsal surface is quite rough, and has many closely interlocked plates, each of which has a strong blunt spine. The entire animal is quite rigid when picked up. The madreporite is generally bright orange, contrasting with the gray color of the rest of the animal. The underside is a yellowish-white with 4 rows of tube feet.

The **purple starfish,** *Asterias vulgaris,* is also found in large numbers in the rocky intertidal area of Cape Ann, often in the same tide pool as the common starfish. However, they can easily be told apart by color, shape and feel. The purple starfish is like its name, purple, but the color may vary a good deal into a bluish tone, pink, rose or even yellowish. The madreporite is always yellow, never orange-red. The shape of the animal is slightly different. The arms are flatter and more pointed. The disc or central portion is crowned and bulges slightly. The plates embedded in the skin are long and narrow,

Purple starfish, *Asterias vulgaris*

and make up a less articulated skeleton than in the common starfish. The animal is therefore flabbier. Its range is from Labrador to Cape Hatteras. South of Cape Cod it is seldom found in the intertidal area, but as one goes north along the coast, the purple star gradually replaces the common starfish as a common inshore animal. Off Cape Ann, the 2 species are about equal in number and are found in the same places.

The brittle stars, Ophiuroidea, (snaky-armed animals) are star-like in shape, with 5 arms, but their resemblance to starfish ends there. They are quite different. There is a small central disc which, except in the basket stars, is never over 2 centimeters in diameter, although the arms may be as much as 10 centimeters long. This disc is flattened, with the mouth and the madreporite on the underside. The arms are thin, many-jointed, and contain no ambulacral groove on the oral side, nor extension of the stomach. The plates in the arms are arranged so that they can move only sideways in the same plane as the disc. However, the arms of the basket star can move in all directions and can meet above the disc, hence the name. The tube feet extend in rows, one on each side of the plates in the arms. They do not have suction cups. The mouth is the center of the disc, and has 5 pairs of long, narrow genital slits through which the sexual products are discharged into the sea. After fertilization, the brittle star hatches into free-swimming larvae which change into small brittle stars which take 3 to 4 years to attain adult size. Brittle stars move by means of their snake-like arms which are also used to catch mollusks, worms, and other small invertebrates for food. A number of brittle stars are found offshore from Cape Ann. Three species may occur on the rocks.

Basket stars are ophiuroids which have hourglass-shaped surfaces on the joints of their arms, permitting them to move vertically as well as horizontally. The arms roll in towards the mouth and over the back. The genital slits are located vertically on the disc at the base of the arms.

The **basket star,** *Gorgonocephalus agassizi,* is generally a deep-water animal, but it can occasionally be found just below the lowest tide mark, among the kelp on the rocky shore of Cape Ann. Frequently, one is brought up by trawlers dragging their nets offshore. It is an extraordinary-looking animal, and unique among the brittle stars because the 5 arms coming off the disc are branched from their base and may branch again. They move in any direction and coil around under themselves, like the handle of a basket. They entwine themselves around any submarine growth. The color and size vary considerably. Discs may range from 5 to 12 centimeters in diameter, with arms from 30 to 45 centimeters long. They may be a chocolate-brown, yellow or cream color.

True brittle stars are flattened and star-shaped. The arms move only in a horizontal plane, and both disc and arms are covered with scale-like plates which may be covered with skin, spines, and granules. The genital pores

Basket star, *Gorgonocephalus agassizi*

are horizontally placed on either side at the base of the arms. Many species occur in deep water. Two are common in the tide pools of Cape Ann.

The **daisy brittle star,** *Ophiopholis aculeata,* has a small disc up to 3 centimeters in diameter, with 10-centimeter arms. It is a colorful animal, quite common in tide pools, among sponges, in the holdfasts of kelp or among the byssal threads of the horse mussels on the rocks of Cape Ann. Its fairly stout arms taper to a fine point, and are often banded. The disc is covered with small spines that conceal some of the plates on top, but not the radial and central plates. Its color varies. There may be a blue star on the disc with green and brown bands on the arms, or a red disc and red-and-white banded arms. The color may be either quite bright or very subdued. Its range is from Long Island to the Arctic.

The **long-armed snake star,** *Amphipholis squamata,* is a small, fragile-looking brittle star with a delicate, very flattened disc about 1 millimeter across, and 5 slender arms, 4 millimeters long, which curl around in a snake-like manner. It is whitish-gray, with a blue tinge. The range is the same as that of the daisy brittle star, and the animals may be told apart by the shape of the dorsal discs or plates on their arms. These discs may be seen clearly with a microscope and may be observed in larger specimens with a ten-power hand lens. The long-armed brittle star has triangular-shaped discs that touch each other at apex and base, all along the arm. The daisy brittle star has blunt oval plates which are separated from each other by a ring of tiny plates. These are visible with a microscope, but the separation of the larger plates can readily be seen with a hand lens.

Sea urchins and sand dollars, Echinoidea, are spiny animals. They have a hard shell or test that completely surrounds the soft parts. Made of rigid plates, the outside of the test is covered with many different kinds of spines that can move in any direction, also pedicellariae and tube feet with suction cups. The tube feet extend through openings in the ambulacral plates. These extend in 5 equally-spaced bands, radiating from the apical plate on the aboral or top of the animal to the oral side where the mouth is located. The area between the tube feet is called the interambulacral zone. There are no openings in these plates, both inter- and ambulacral zones have spines and pedicellariae. These pedicellariae are pincer-like protuberances on flexible stalks that are used for picking debris off the animal, as well as for organs of defense. Some excrete an irritating poison. The apical plate is surrounded by 5 central plates, one of which is the madreporite, and 5 smaller ocular plates with eye spots. Below, the mouth parts, known as Aristotle's lantern, are set in the center of the shell. It consists of a large number of pieces culminating

Daisy brittle star, *Ophiopholis aculeata*

in 5 pointed teeth whose points come together like a beak, and which, with complex muscles, can open and grab things like the jaws of a steam shovel.

An inside body cavity or coelom surrounds the soft parts. There is a ring canal directly connected to the madreporite. Inside this ring canal the intestinal tract opens from the mouth, goes up for a short distance, then curves right around the coelom and finally empties to the outside through the anus, which is located in the apical plate. 5 large gonads lie between the rows of tube feet. In some of the echinoids a gonad may not be apparent, but in the sea urchin or sand dollar they are usually prominent. The sexes are separate, and sea urchins collect near shore several times a year when they are ready to spawn. At these times, the swollen gonads make delicious eating, especially appreciated in southern Europe, in Chile, and in the tropics. Sea urchins and sand dollars go through a complicated double metamorphosis after hatching that includes two free-swimming larval stages.

Because of their hard parts, like the mollusks, echinoderms are often found as fossils. These animals have been known since the Ordovician Period, nearly 2 billion years ago. A study of their development through the geologic ages has produced much knowledge of the interrelationship of the various groups of echinoderms. Sea urchins are represented by one species on the rocky shores of Cape Ann. Sand dollars are present on our sandy areas.

The **green sea urchin,** *Strongylocentrotus dröbachiensis* is the common
sea urchin found on all our Cape Ann rocks. It ranges around the Arctic,
being found in northern Europe and the northern Pacific, as well as in eastern
Canada. Cape Cod is the southern limit of these species. From there to the
Caribbean it is replaced by the purple sea urchin, *Arbacia punctulata,* which is
the great source of embryological material studied in laboratories. Our green
sea urchin is a squat, spherical animal somewhat flattened, completely and
thickly covered with rather blunt spines and tubercules. There is no bare area
anywhere. The tubercules are set in distinct vertical lines. The test may be up
to 10 centimeters in diameter, and the spines are generally 2 centimeters
long. Found in tide pools, in rock crevices, and under seaweed, they are
often jammed in so tightly that it is hard to remove them. The tube feet of
this species have suction cups which secure it tightly and it is able to withstand being swept away and smashed by waves.

The **common sand dollar,** *Echinarachnius parma,* has a circular test that is
flat and thin and about 8 centimeters in diameter. It is covered with fine
spines. The mouth is on the underside and the anal opening is at the edge
of the shell. Radiating from the center of the aboral or upper side of the test
are 5 ambulacral areas which correspond to the arms of the starfish, and the
same areas that curve around the bulge of a sea urchin. They look like petals
open at the end and are easy to see when a sand dollar is found dead on a
beach and the spines have been rubbed off. The mouth is on the underside
in the center. The anus is at the edge of the test. In the water, the animal is a
purplish-brown, but turns greenish when exposed to the air. The sand dollar
lives on sandy bottoms in about 5 meters of water, and occurs in huge numbers
in certain places. The bottom may seem paved with them, or they may not be
present at all. They seem to be distributed in a random manner on the bottom.
They usually bury themselves just under the top layer of sand but also rest
completely exposed on the bottom in the water. Flounders, cod, and haddock
feed on sand dollars. A large colony of sand dollars can lie off a beach un-
discovered because the only evidence of their presence is the dead ones washed
ashore, and this can happen only occasionally after a big storm. The dead
shells are fragile and break to pieces easily. They are common north from
New Jersey and in certain sandy areas in Gloucester Harbor, the Annisquam
River, and Ipswich Bay around Cape Ann.

Sea cucumbers, holothurians, are somewhat different from other echinoderms. They are bag-like creatures, much elongated and designed to creep

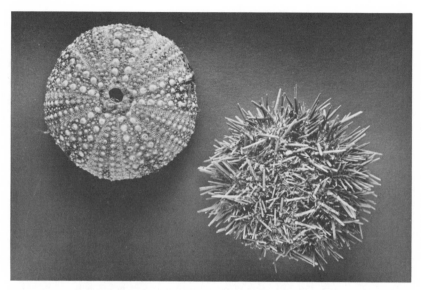

Green sea urchin, *Strongylocentrotus dröbachiensis*, with and without spines

Common sand dollar, *Echinarachnius parma*, without spines

along the bottom of the sea or to burrow in mud or sand. Usually the 5-part symmetry on the outside of the animal is hard to see at first glance. One must look at a sea cucumber head-on to see the radial arrangement of 5 equally spaced longitudinal rows of tube feet, and 5 or 10 sets of tentacles arranged around the mouth. The 2 upper rows of tube feet do not have suckers like the 3 lower ones, but are adapted for respiration and recording sensations. There is no test or even large plates in the skin of the holothurians, but many intricately designed small plates are scattered about in their thick skin. The plates rarely articulate and seldom are close enough to actually stiffen the body wall. The animals move by strongly contracting their muscular bodies and hitching along the bottom.

Sea cucumbers have an interesting mechanism for breathing called respiratory trees. These are long many-branched tubes which extend the entire length of the body from the cloaca, the place where the intestine empties itself, inside the body cavity on each side of the digestive tract. Breathing is accomplished by seawater being forced through these trees by powerful contractions of the cloaca. Oxygen is removed from the circulating seawater. The pulsating movement of this process may be seen in most of the sea cucumbers.

Holothurians have a water-vascular system, which controls the tube feet and tentacles, similar to that in the other classes of echinoderms, with a ring canal, a stone canal and a madreporite which opens into the body cavity instead of directly to the outside. The ring canal also opens into the 5 ambulacral tubes that run the entire length of the body and connects with the tube feet outside. The sexes are separate in most sea cucumbers and there is a single gonad that discharges its sex product into the sea through a duct situated dorsally behind the ring of tentacles. After fertilization the eggs hatch into free-swimming larvae that change into tiny sea cucumbers. Like certain other echinoderms, holothurians have great regenerative power.

There are many species of holothurians found all over the world in cold, temperate, and tropical waters, but only two are apt to be found off Cape Ann.

The large **northern sea cucumber**, *Cucumaria frondosa*, has a thick-walled cylindrical body, somewhat narrower at each end, just like a cucumber. It is reddish-brown in color. There are 5 radial lines of tube feet evenly spaced around the animal, and 10 branching tree-like tentacles. It may be 30 centimeters long, although it is often considerably smaller. It lives in cold tide pools or rocky areas near the low-tide line, from Nantucket northward. It is common on the coast of Maine, in the colder waters, and has been found on the rocky shores off Cape Ann.

Northern sea cucumber, *Cucumaria frondosa*

The **burrowing sea cucumber,** *Leptosynapta tenuis,* is a translucent worm-like animal that lives buried in sand or clear mud along the Atlantic coast from Maine to South Carolina. Its length varies from 12 to 18 centimeters in size and its color from whitish or yellow tinged with pink. The internal organs and the 4 longitudinal muscles can be seen through the translucent body walls. There is a ring of many-branched tentacles surrounding the mouth. These animals live in burrows in sand or mud and sometimes may be found exposed

Burrowing sea cucumber, *Leptosynapta tenuis*

at low tide when the sand is still wet. The burrows may be spotted when you are snorkeling by the presence of small mounds of fine sand with a hole at the center. They live in sheltered areas rather than places exposed to waves.

Moss animals — phylum Bryozoa

This phylum is made up of many very small colonial animals that live on rocks, algae, shells, wharf pilings, etc. All need magnification in order to study them. Some colonies are stalked; some are encrusting. They are included here because they are common and are found on all the rocky shores of Cape Ann.

The **tufted bryozoan,** *Bugula turrita,* is a stalked form that may grow up to 35 centimeters in length, though usually much less. It has many branches made up of flat, fan-like, limy plates each of which contains an animal. Although usually pale yellow in color, it may be orange. It ranges from Casco Bay to North Carolina, and is found in short tufts on the rocks of Cape Ann. It is easily confused with dead or dying branching coralline algae.

Tufted bryozoan, *Bugula turrita*

Sea lace, *Membranipora* sp. is an encrusting bryozoan often found in whitish patches on algae or shells and occasionally on rocks. Examine the colony in seawater carefully with a magnifying glass. Often the tiny calcareous cells are empty, but sometimes live colonies may be found near the low-tide mark. One can see the animal open and put out delicate tentacles and sweep the water like a barnacle feeding. This is a close-knit colony with oval windows or trapdoors in each cell. It is found all around Cape Ann on rocky shores or cast up on beaches.

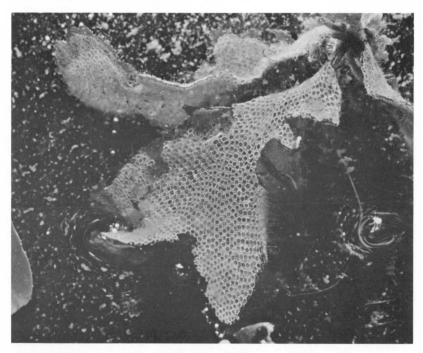

Sea lace, *Membranipora* sp.

Vertebrates
The chordates — phylum Chordata (animals with a nerve cord)

This is the last and most advanced phylum from an evolutionary point of view. It includes vertebrates (animals with backbones) and protochordates, the invertebrates (animals with no backbone) that bridge the gap to higher animals. These protochordates have structures either in larval or adult stages that forecast the characteristics of a vertebrate, which are: 1) a notochord 2) a dorsal nerve cord with a neural canal 3) a series of paired gill slits and 4) a ventral mouth and anus. Not all the protochordates have all these characteristics, and some have them only in the larval stage. Certainly none of them look much like the classes of vertebrates: cyclostomes, (lampreys and hagfishes), fishes, amphibians, reptiles, birds and mammals.

Sea squirts, class Ascidiacea, are animals shaped like a wine skin. The ascidians or sea squirts are so called because they are usually of a bulbous shape with 2 conspicuous spouts or siphons which eject water when the animal is disturbed. The larval forms of sea squirts are entirely different from the adult stage. The larva is bilaterally symmetrical and elongated, looking much more like a tadpole than the adult sea potato or sea vase that we know. It has a ventral mouth, a brain lying dorsally between mouth and anus or excurrent siphon, a dorsal nerve cord, below that a notochord or stiffening rod, and paired gill slits. As the animal develops, the intestines curl around and the notochord and the dorsal nerve cord disappear. The gill slits move closer together and only these gill clefts remain to show its relationship to the larva. The internal organization of these animals is completely hidden by the thick tunic or skin. Sometimes this is transparent and internal parts may be distinguished with a hand lens. The circulatory system of the ascidians is remarkable for the ability of the heart to reverse the direction of the flow of blood around the animals at frequent intervals. This can be observed in a transparent individual under the microscope or with a very strong hand lens.

Sea pork, *Amaroucium* sp., is a colonial sea squirt with a thick gelatinous slimy covering that suggests a mass of salt pork. It feels slippery. Often it is found on wharf pilings and on the walls of sea caves or under rocks and on rock overhangs. It encrusts the substrate at or near the low-tide mark. It may be 3 centimeters thick. There are various species ranging south from New England.

The sea vase, *Ciona intestinalis*, is a tall, slender, single transparent individual of golden-yellow color with the 2 siphon openings close together at the top. The intestines show as a rounded mass at the base of the animal with a tube extending up one side but not quite connecting with the lower siphon. It is found on submerged wharf piles or on rocks and is 5 to 8 centimeters in length. It occurs all along the New England coast.

The star tunicate or colonial ascidian, *Botryllus schlosseri*, is an encrusting species of varying thickness found under rocks, on boat bottoms, wharf pilings, eelgrass, etc., often enveloping a frond of Irish moss or *Gigartina*. Examine these species with a magnifying lens, and the stars which are situated in the

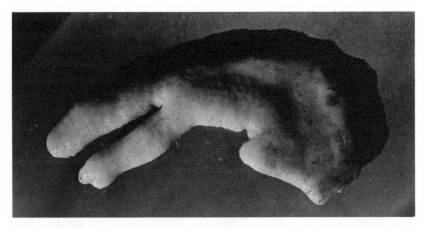

Sea pork, *Amaroucium* sp.

Sea vase, *Ciona intestinalis*

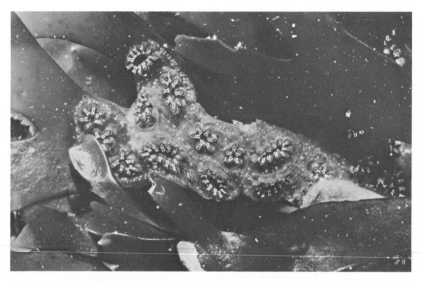

Star tunicate, *Botryllus schlosseri*

gelatinous mass will be seen to be composed of individual animals clustered together in a definite arrangement of round or oval groups. These clusters are often green in a yellowish background. They are common from Massachusetts south.

The **sea potato** or stalked ascidian, *Boltenia ovifera,* is a bright red ascidian that grows offshore on a slender stalk up to 20 centimeters long in about 15 meters of water. The body of this animal looks like a shrunken, shriveled, deformed carrot or potato. It is about the size of a duck egg, oval, with two blunt protuberances that are the siphons. This animal is often found from eastern Canada to Cape Cod on exposed beaches cast up with various seaweeds after a storm. The farther north one goes, the shallower the water where one finds the sea potato.

Sea grapes, *Molgula* sp., are often found in the Cape Ann area growing in bunches on rocks, piles, under docks or floating objects such as timbers, buoys, mooring lines, on the bottom of boats. It is characteristic of shallow water. Each animal is about 3 centimeters or less in diameter. It is a round, gelatinous globule with two distinct well-separated tubes opening to the outside. Though the body of a sea grape is translucent, it is often covered with a brownish deposit that makes its shape hard to distinguish. Sometimes they are covered by a colony of *Botryllus schlosseri,* the star tunicate. There are many species of *Molgula* that live all along the western Atlantic. It is impossible to determine the specific animal without microscopic investigation.

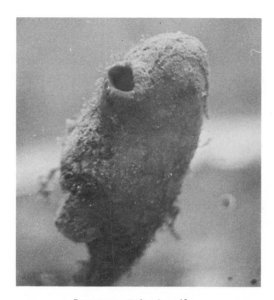

Sea potato, *Boltenia ovifera*

Sea grapes, *Molgula* sp.

Marine fishes of Cape Ann and adjacent waters

A fish is a vertebrate, an animal with a backbone, especially adapted for living in water. These creatures are made up of many cells which group together and form such complicated systems as the muscular, skeletal, nervous, reproductive, digestive and circulatory systems. Fish are equipped with features that enable them to survive within an aquatic world.

The characteristics of fish are:

1. Fins — these structures fall under two categories: paired and unpaired. Just to the rear of the skull, are the paired; and the unpaired are dorsal (top), anal, and caudal (tail) fins. Fins prevent fish from rolling over and enable them to effectively move ahead as well as up and down, and even stop. Many fish have modified fins which are used to feel around and even attract prey.

2. Scales are a part of the skeletal system, and are possessed by most fishes. Pipefish and sturgeons have bony plates as a scale substitute. The little shields act as barriers and protect fish from harmful bacteria and viruses. The scales' smooth surface reduces drag and allows fish to swim along swiftly within the water. Biologists can determine the age of some fish by examining its scales under a microscope. At the end of each growing season, an annulus or growth ring is laid down on the scale's periphery. The number of growth rings reveal the age.

3. Gills — instead of lungs, fishes are equipped with gills. These sensitive structures come in direct contact with the water and release carbon dioxide as well as take in oxygen. The gills of living fishes are always red because of constantly circulating blood, which is responsible for the transferral of oxygen to the many cells in the body. The operculars, special lid-like bones on each side of the skull, cover and protect the gills.

4. Shape — according to area inhabited, fish body forms are specialized. For bottom-dwellers like skates and flounders, their bodies are flattened from top to bottom, and their eyes are located on the top side. Frequently, the pectoral fins are enlarged and wing-like. Such a plate-like form allows the creature to settle in the sediment and be as inconspicuous as possible. In contrast, those that live within the water column tend to have elongated bodies with pointed noses, tapered posterior ends, and deeply forked tail fins. Such a body permits a fish to pass easily through the water. The deeply forked tail can be vigorously flapped back and forth without using up a great deal of energy as would a rounded caudal fin.

5. Color — another manner in which fish are specialized is by body colorations. As a general rule, most fish closely resemble their surroundings in color. For the near-surface inhabitants, their tops are bluish-green, as

water appears from above. Their silvery underparts blend with water and sky as seen from below. Such blending in colorations allows many fish to escape would-be predators. On the other hand, bottom-dwellers closely mimic the colors of the sediment which they live on. The winter flounder spends most of its time on a muddy bottom; its back is brownish-black. The yellowtail flounder lives on the sand, and its topside is tan with brown and black speckles. The rarely-seen bellies are white. In a few instances, fish advertise their presence by bright colors so as to purposely attract predators. The silver, brown-blotched colored Portuguese man-of-war fish swims amongst the poisonous tentacles of the Portuguese man-of-war jelly-fish. The little fish, immune to the poison, attracts predators which in turn fall victim to the jellyfish.

Thousands upon thousands of fish species live in the earth's waters. Strangely enough, these creatures fall under three categories. The most primitive group are the Agnatha or jawless fishes. Lampreys and hagfishes are its members, which lack jaws, bony skeletons, and paired fins. Eel-like lampreys live off other fishes by sucking their blood. Hagfishes are blind.

The next category is the cartilaginous fishes, Chondrichthyes. These are the orders Selachii (sharks) and Batoideii (rays), which have true jaws, cartilaginous skeletons, and paired fins. A shark's skin is covered by special placoid scales, which have structures identical to teeth. The scales are responsible for a shark's rough, sandpapery skin.

The final and most advanced group are the bony fishes, Osteichthyes. These fish have true jaws and paired fins in addition to their bony skeletons. Being the most numerous and successful of all the fishes, these fish live in fresh, salty, and even brackish waters. All three categories are represented in our waters. Many of the fishes do not live at their inshore homes during the winter months. Extremely harsh environmental conditions either force the fishes to deeper water or to more southerly locations. But, the deep-water dwellers often do a lot of traveling either in search of food or of spawning grounds.

The **cunner,** *Tautogolabrus adspersus,* 5 to 40 centimeters, is a common tenant of the rocky seaweed-covered bottom. These deep-bodied, often reddish-brown fish travel in and out with the tides, and gather in large numbers when food is around. For the rocky-shore fisherman, the thick-skinned bony cunner is a certain catch.

The **tautog,** *Tautoga onitis,* is a close cunner relative. Often swimming with its cousin cunner, this fish has powerful jaws and many teeth used for cracking thick mussel and crab shells.

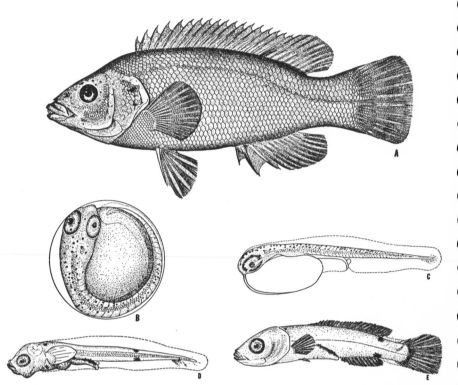

Cunner (*Tautogolabrus adspersus*).   A, adult, Woods Hole, Mass.; from Goode, drawing by H. L. Todd. B, egg; C, larva, newly hatched, 2.2 mm.; D, larva, 4.2 mm.; E, young, 8 mm. B–E, after Kuntz and Radcliffe.

Cunner, *Tautogolabrus adspersus*

The **sea raven,** *Hemitripterus americanus,* is a not so common, unusual looking fish, often nicknamed daddy grouper. When it wants to make itself fearful to frighten away intruders, the sea raven can puff itself up by filling its stomach with water. The creature has prickly, warty skin, and varies in color from brick-red to yellow. The fin tips have seaweed-like fleshy lobes which further camouflage the fish on the bottom.

The **codfish,** *Gadus callarias,* is a round-bodied fish which occasionally lives within the rocky, shallow-water area. Like its haddock and pollock brothers, the cod has three distinct dorsal fins. Its body color is either olive-green, or as with the rock cod, reddish-brown. This fish grows to a length of 2 meters, and has a reputation of being vicious and feeding on anything in sight.

The **rock eel,** *Pholis gunnellus,* which is not an eel at all, is often found in tide pools of the Kelp Zone. Sometimes they are under rocks on a rocky shore. They blend into their surroundings and curve around whatever algae

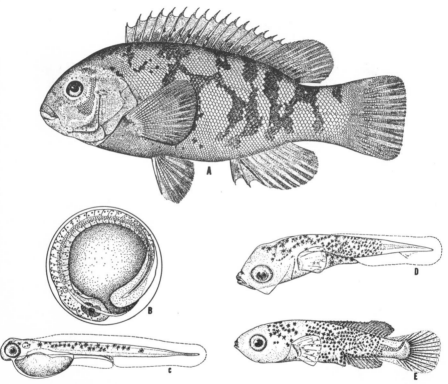

Tautog. *Tautoga onitis*. A, adult, Woods Hole, Mass.; from Goode, drawing by H. L. Todd. B, egg; C, larva, one day old, 2.9 mm.; D, larva, 5 mm.; E, young fry, 10 mm. B–E, after Kuntz and Radcliffe.

Tautog, *Tautoga onitis*

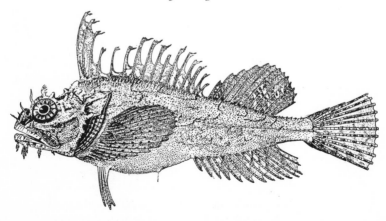

Sea raven, *Hemitripterus americanus*

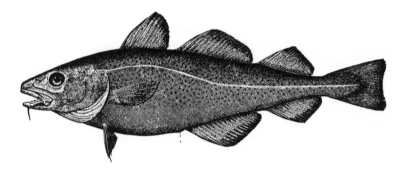

Codfish, *Gadus callarias*

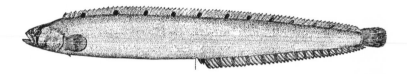

Rock eel, *Pholis gunnellus*

or rocks are present so that they are hard to see. They are wiggly and slippery so that they are hard to catch. If possible, put one of these fish in a plastic container and watch it for a while. It is spindle-shaped with a seemingly continuous fin running from just about the line of the gill right around the tail to a point about midway from mouth to tail. There seems to be practically no caudal peduncle. Black-centered, pale-edged spots are spaced at equal intervals along the back and dorsal fin and contrast with the yellow to red to brown coloring of the animal. Rock eels can be 20 to 25 centimeters in length. Those in tide pools are rarely 12 centimeters long. These are fish of rocks and pebbles, not mud or eelgrass, so are found in the truly rocky areas of the Cape Ann coast. They range all around the northern Atlantic from Delaware Bay to Hudson Strait. They are more numerous in colder water.

The **radiated shanny,** *Ulvaria subbifurcata,* is another little fish which lives under the rocks near the low-tide line. This creature's body form is similar to the rock eel's except for being a bit stouter. The shanny is brown-colored, and on each side of its skull near the eyes, is a black diagonal bar.

The **sea snail,** *Neoliparis atlanticus,* is an unusual fish which looks very similar to the tadpole. This is the olive-green colored sea snail. The tiny 6- to 15-centimeter fish has pelvic fins which are modified and form a ventral sucking disc. The disc allows the fish to cling to rocks and even buoys.

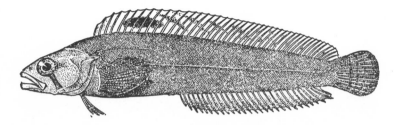

Radiated shanny, *Ulvaria subbifurcata*

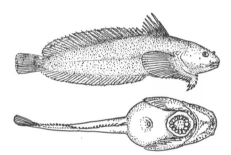

Sea snail, *Neoliparis atlanticus*

The **blackback flounder,** *Pseudopleuronectes americanus* is the most common flounder. The winter flounder or blackback frequently swims into very shallow water in search of sea worms and moves in and out with the tides. Often, the young remain in sandy beach tide pools and cover themselves as best as possible with sand. The winter flounder can regulate the degree of color darkness on its topside.

The **yellowtail flounder,** *Limanda ferruginea,* is another common flatfish that usually lives in deeper waters than its thicker-bodied cousin, the blackback. Besides having a sandy-colored, speckled back, this fish has a yellow-colored patch near its tail.

Another interesting sandy-colored, paper-thin flatfish is the **windowpane flounder,** *Lophopsetta maculata.* When held up to the light, this plate-shaped flounder can be nearly transparent. Fishermen call these unmarketable fish see-through flounder.

A few cartilaginous fishes live in the sandy bottom area. Most common is the little **skate,** *Raja erinacea,* which occasionally gets washed ashore on beaches. This fish uses its wing-like pectoral fins for moving about and for stirring up sand which acts as body camouflage.

Blackback flounder, *Pseudopleuronectes americanus*

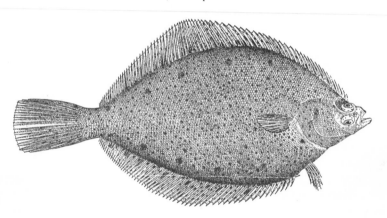

Yellowtail flounder, *Limanda ferruginea*

Longhorn sculpins, *Myoxocephalus octodecimspinosus,* are very abundant. The 20- to 35-centimeter fish, white with yellow and black splotches have extremely long and stiff cheekbone and dorsal fin spines. One can get a good stabbing if not careful while unhooking these fish. Unlike many fish, this sculpin can make grunting noises when handled.

Another unusual creature is the **ocean pout,** *Macrozoarces americanus,* also called congo eel, mutton fish, and even blubber lips. This eel-like olive-green fish has a big head with thick fleshy lips. Its jaws are powerful and

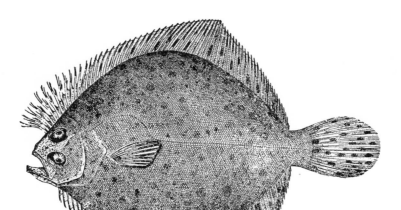

Windowpane flounder, *Lophopsetta maculata*

armed with many cone-shaped teeth, many of which are green-colored. This 30- to 90-centimeter fish is one of the few that feeds on sand dollars.

The **sand launces**, *Ammodytes americanus*, are small and pin-shaped. They travel in dense schools and are favorite food for many predatory fishes. As an escape mechanism, sand launces can quickly burrow several inches under the sand.

The **anglerfish**, or American goosefish, *Lophius americanus* is called monk-fish. Besides being flat and large-mouthed, the creature's brown-colored flesh has no scales. Instead, it is protected by a thin layer of slimy mucous. The first dorsal fin spine is modified into a special lure structure. While lying partially buried within the mud, the fish flaps its lure up and down. Curious fish are attracted, and when they get close enough, the monkfish plunges forward with its mouth wide open and swallows a victim or two. Its jaws are equipped with long conical teeth which all point inward. Also, the fish has no ribs, which allows it to gulp down large objects. Anglerfish have a reputation for surfacing and swallowing ducks.

The **squirrel hake**, *Urophycis chuss*, is another interesting fish. It is some-times known as red hake. In some areas, red or squirrel hake cover the bottom like herds of cattle browsing in pastures. Similar to the ocean pout, hakes have long dorsal and anal fins. Their pelvic fins form thread-like appendages

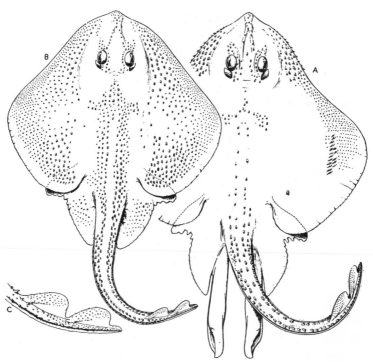

Little skate (*Raja erinacea*).   A, male, 20 inches long, Boston Harbor; B, female, 17½ inches long, Mystic Connecticut; C, side view, end of tail of same, about 0.6 times natural size.   From Bigelow and Schroeder.   Drawings by E. N. Fischer.

Skate, *Raja erinacea*

Longhorn sculpin, *Myoxocephalus octodecimspinosus*

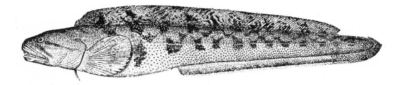

Ocean pout, *Macrozoarces americanus*

Sand launce, *Ammodytes americanus*

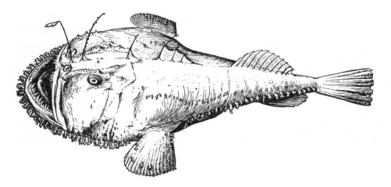

Anglerfish, *Lophius americanus*

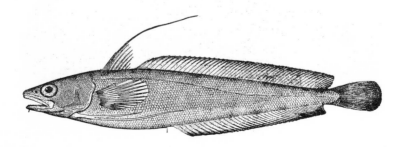

Squirrel hake, *Urophycis chuss*

used for feeling around on the bottom. The hake's body is pale brown with a yellow belly. Because of the underside color, squirrel hake are often called butterballs. Young 6- to 10-centimeter hake hide in the strangest places. Sea scallops often provide shelters for the small fish. It is reputed that 1 scallop out of 8 has a tiny hake inside.

The **common mummichog**, *Fundulus heteroclitus*, or killifish, and the **striped mummichog**, *Fundulus majalis*, are both found all around Cape Ann. They are small fish up to 12 centimeters in length, but usually smaller. They are stout-bodied with a blunt nose and a rounded tail and very wide between tail and body. Both are a murky greenish color on top with a whitish or yellow belly. The common mummichog is a stouter more massive fish than the striped mummy, which is more slender and has stripes which are vertical in the male and horizontal in the female, at all stages of life. *F. heteroclitus* has stripes only in the breeding season. Both mummichogs are found along the shore and in intertidal areas, especially in estuaries and marshy areas where they collect in large numbers at low tide in the shallow water in the bottom of creeks and in watery pockets in the marshes. These fish are very resistant to the lack of oxygen. They can live out of water for as long as 2 hours and if stranded in a pool that dries up, they will work their way into the mud and wait for high tide. Mummichogs are as at home in the brackish water as in normal salt water. They range from the Gulf of St. Lawrence to Florida. The striped mummichog is more common in the waters of southern New England, but both are common around Cape Ann.

The **sticklebacks**, *Gasterosteus* sp. are small fish up to 10 centimeters in

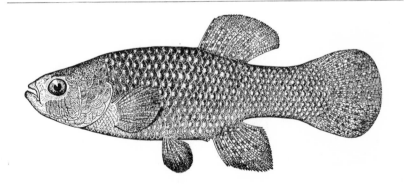

Common mummichog, *Fundulus heteroclitus*

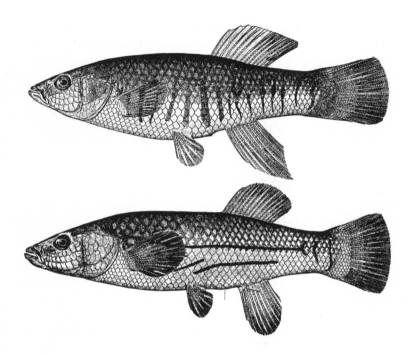

Striped mummichog, *Fundulus majalis*

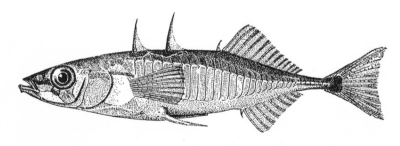

Sticklebacks, *Gasterosteus* sp.

length with two or more stout spines on their back in front of the dorsal fin which is located quite near the tail. They have a fan-shaped tail and a very narrow caudal peduncle. In color the sticklebacks vary from greenish-gray to olive-brown or blue on top with a silvery belly. In spring, breeding time, both males and females turn red. The females turn red all over except on the back, while the males turn red on the underparts from mouth to anus with occasional spots on the sides. Like the mummichogs, these are shore fish and equally at home in salt or brackish water all around Cape Ann. They are often found in the upper tide pools of the rocky shores in the spring washed up by high tides. They may breed there and young can be found in July, but by August the pools have dried up or become quite foul. The young are doomed, as there are no high tides to refresh the pools or wash the fry out to sea. The males actually build nests of pieces of grass for the females to lay eggs in. They often school beneath floats and piers. Sticklebacks are common in the Gulf of Maine. They range from Cape Cod to the Bay of Fundy.

Another estuary inhabitant is the **pipefish**, *Syngnathus fuscus.* This slender, 12- to 15-centimeter pencil-shaped fish lives way up in the marshes and wraps its body around marsh grass and eelgrass. The small

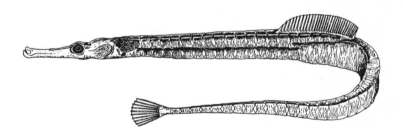

Pipefish, *Syngnathus fuscus*

creature has bony plates instead of scales, and a long snout which it uses to suck in victims. The **seahorse**, *Hippocampus hudsonius,* is a close relative, and is occasionally found off Cape Ann.

The **tomcod**, *Microgadus tomcod,* are also called frostfish, and are very numerous. These fish look exactly like the Atlantic cod, but are much smaller and have more blotched color patterns.

The **American eel**, *Anguilla rostrata,* can be found living in harbors and estuaries during the spring and fall months. These creatures have a very complex life cycle. All of the eel spawning is done during midwinter in the depths of the Sargasso Sea, off Bermuda. The parent eels die after spawning. The eggs later

Seahorse, *Hippocampus hudsonius*

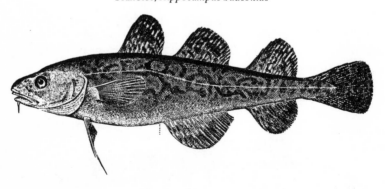

Tomcod, *Microgadus tomcod*

float to the near surface and develop into ribbon-like transparent forms. Currents carry the tiny fish inland, and by this time, the creatures have become small eels or elvers. The males of these tiny snake-like fish remain

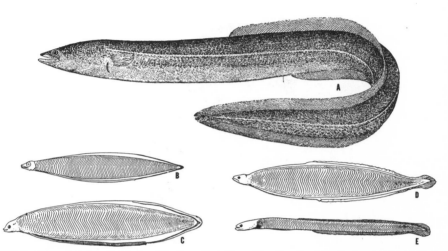

Eel (*Anguilla rostrata*). A, adult, Connecticut River, Massachusetts; from Goode, drawing by H. L. Todd; B, "Leptocephalus" stage, 49 mm.; C, "Leptocephalus" stage, 55 mm.; D, "Leptocephalus" stage, 58 mm.; E, transformation stage, 61 mm. B–E, after Schmidt.

American eel, *Anguilla rostrata*

under rocks and seaweeds within the intertidal zone, while the females find their way into fresh water quarries and ponds. When these fish become adults, they leave the fresh water in the fall and begin the long journey to the breeding grounds.

The **wolffish,** *Anarhichas lupus*, has a deep body, colored gray with black vertical bands running along its sides. Most interesting is the fish's teeth. The creature mainly feeds on shellfish. Its front teeth are chisel-like and are used for prying off mussels from rocks. To the rear of its mouth are upper and lower rounded, crushing teeth which crack shells to pieces. This fish has bitten many fishermen's boots while on deck.

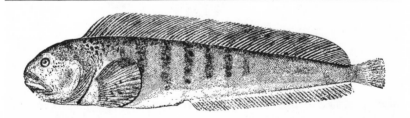

Wolffish, *Anarhichas lupus*

The **redfish** or ocean perch, *Sebastes marinus,* frequently lives on the tops of underwater rocky hills or rises. This fish looks similar to the cunner, but has a deeper body, many stiff spines, large bulgy eyes, and a red color. Redfish can only be caught during the day because during the night, the creatures leave the bottom in search of food.

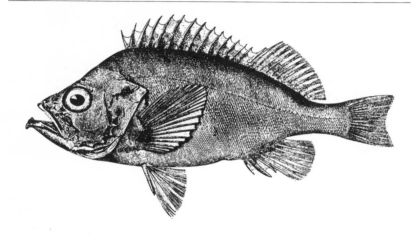

Redfish, *Sebastes marinus*

Hauling back the trawl

Bringing the trawl aboard the Judith Lee Rose

Beachcombing

Last year's growth of thatch grass cast upon beach

Goose-necked barnacle, *Lepas fascicularis,* native in warmer waters, but occasionally transported north.

Operculum (device to close shell) of common northern moon snail, *Lunatia heros*

Wood bored by *Teredo* "worms"; the organisms are bivalve mollusks.

Egg case of little skate, *Raja* sp.

Harbor seal, *Phoca vitulina*

Recommended Reading

Bigelow, Henry, 1926. PLANKTON OF THE OFFSHORE WATERS OF THE GULF OF MAINE, Harvard University Document 968, Cambridge, Mass. 509 pp. A technical and thorough study of the 1900's. Of unsurpassed excellence.

Carson, Rachael, 1955. THE EDGE OF THE SEA, Houghton Mifflin Co., Boston. Enjoyable introduction to the organisms living at the edge of the sea. Available in paperback. 276 pp.

Dawson, E. Yale, 1966. MARINE BOTANY — AN INTRODUCTION, Holt, Rinehart and Winston, Inc., New York. 317 pp. Textbook survey of major forms of marine algae.

Kingsbury, John M., 1970. THE ROCKY SHORE, The Chatham Press, Inc., Chatham, Mass. 77 pp. Charming informative series of essays on nature study.

MacGinitie, G. E. and N. MacGinitie, 1968. NATURAL HISTORY OF MARINE ANIMALS, McGraw-Hill Book Co. A wealth of information in usable style, 523 pp.

Miner, R. W., 1950. FIELD BOOK OF SEASHORE LIFE, G. P. Putnam's Sons. 888 pp. A complete guide for the animals of eastern coast of the United States.

Smith, Ralph, 1964. KEYS TO MARINE INVERTEBRATES OF THE WOODS HOLE REGION, Systematics-Ecology Program, Contribution No. 11, 208 pp. Technical but highly useful key.

Teal, John and Mildred Teal, 1969, LIFE AND DEATH OF THE SALT MARSH, Audubon/Ballantine Book, New York, 274 pp. A well-detailed and comprehensive account of the ecology of the salt marsh. Well suited for the layman. Available in paperback.

Yonge, C. M., 1949. THE SEA SHORE, Collins New Naturalist, London, England, 311 pp. Intended for British Isles, but equally useful for cold waters of North America. Splendid. Available in paperback.

Glossary

aboral	away from mouth
abyssal	pertaining to depths of the ocean
algae	lower plants that can photosynthesize
algin	a material obtained from certain algae; when dry is hard and when moist is slimy; alginate is a salt from algin
alternation of generations	each generation or age group acts and looks different from its parents but the same as its grandparents
ambulacral	pertaining to the grooves in certain echinoderms from which the tube feet project
ammonia	colorless gaseous compound of nitrogen and hydrogen, NH_3, lighter than air and of extremely strong smell and taste
anaerobic	free of oxygen; an anaerobe is an organism that can live without oxygen
antenna	whip-like paired appendage of Crustacea; pl. antennae
anterior	front
anus	opening of the digestive system to the exterior at opposite end from the mouth
aperture	opening
apical	pertaining to the top
articulate	jointed
ascidean	member of the phylum Chordata; the sea squirts
asexual reproduction	reproduction or formation of a new individual by the division, spore-forming, fission or budding of one parent cell; the new individual therefore was originally part of the parent
bacteria	large group of microscopic plants which usually do not photosynthesize
beta carotene	an orange fat-soluble plant pigment such as is found in carrots
biliproteins	a blue or reddish water-soluble plant pigment
bioluminescence	light caused by combination of two chemicals produced by an organism's body
biomass	total weight of organisms in a set area
bivalve	an animal with a shell of two parts hinged together
black zone	layer of blue-green alga, *Calothrix,* occurring at high-tide line
bloom	an extreme growth in the numbers of phytoplankton, characteristic of spring and fall

149

blue-green algae	algae of the phylum Cyanophyta
brackish	pertaining to water that is a mixture of salt and fresh
breaker	a wave breaking into foam against the shore, a sandbar, or against a rock or reef near the surface
brown algae	algae of the phylum Phaeophyta
buccal	of the mouth
calcareous	containing calcium
calcite	a mineral made up of calcium and oxygen
calcium carbonate	$CaCO_3$, found in limestone, chalk, marble, plant ashes, bones and in many shells
carapace	shell as in a turtle or arthropod
carnivorous	meat-eating
carotene	a yellow pigment made by plants and found in milk, liver, oils, egg yolk
carotenoids	general group of pigments found in plants and some animal tissues
caudal	having to do with the tail
cellulose	a carbohydrate forming the main part of the cell walls of plants
cell wall	non-living material that surrounds the cell of most plants
cephalothorax	head and thorax segments often fused in arthropods holder; a stone whirled about on the end of a string exerts centrifugal force on the string
cephalothorax	head and thorax segments often fused in arthropods
cephalic	pertaining to the head
chlorophyll	the green plant pigment found in all photosynthesizing plants
Chlorophyta	a phylum of lower plants including the green algae
chloroplast	a tiny grain within the plant cell that contains the chlorophyll pigments
cilia	hair-like flexible growths on the surface of cells
cirrus	flexible appendage of an animal; pl. cirri
class	a subdivision of a major phylum
classification	art of distributing into groups, classes or families
cloaca	end part of the gut in certain invertebrates especially sea cucumbers
coelom	body cavity derived by splitting of the mesoderm
colonial	a group of plants or animals living together
columella	the central column of a shell about which the whorls are coiled
concave	bending inward
continental shelf	a shallow underwater plain bordering the continents, that varies in width from several to several hundred miles, usually ending with a continental slope
continental slope	the usually steep slope from a continental shelf to the ocean depths
cord (nerve)	a hollow tube with a very small hole containing nerve fibers, as in spinal cord

Crustacea	a class of the phylum Arthropoda, mostly marine, characterized by a hard outer skin or shell
currents	the part of a fluid body that moves continuously in a certain direction; can be either air or water
Cyanophyta	a phylum of lower plants; the blue-green algae
cyclostome	one of a class of fish like the lamprey
debris	an accumulation of detached fragments
density	the mass of a substance per unit volume
desiccation	the removal of water from a substance
detritus	any product of disintegration
diatom	a unicellular form of algae with walls of silica
dinoflagellate	a small plankton with two flagella
distilled water	water free of any mineral matter
diurnal	occurring every day
diversity	having differences and variety
dorsal	pertaining to the back
ebb	the flowing back of the tide towards the sea
elliptical	oval
elytra	scale of an annelid worm or wing of insect
environment	all the external influences that affect an organism
epidermis	outer layer of an animal's skin
estuary	a place where tide water and river water meet
evaporation	the process by which any substance is changed from a liquid into vapor
eviscerate	to disembowel; to take out the intestines
exoskeleton	a hard, supporting or protective structure on the outside of a body like the shell of a crustacean
feces	waste products eliminated from the body through the alimentary canal
filamentous	thread-like
fission	the division of one cell, or a unicellular organism into two or more parts
fjord	a narrow, deep inlet of the sea
flagella	long flexible hairs on the surface of certain organisms; move like a whip to push the organism forward
foot	a muscular organ of locomotion in mollusks
fossil	remains of a plant or animal turned to stone or the imprint of the remains
fragmentation	division by splitting or breaking into parts
fucoxanthin	the main pigment in brown algae besides chlorophyll
gamete	sexual cells; a mature germ cell such as sperm or egg that can form a new cell by joining with another gamete
ganglia	small masses of nervous tissue connecting cell bodies
gastropod	a snail
genital	pertaining to reproduction

genus	a category of plants and animals that includes closely related species
gill	organ for extracting oxygen from water
gonad	sexual organ
gram	a metric unit of mass and weight equal to one cubic centimeter of freshwater at its maximum density at 4°C
gravity	the force of attraction of all bodies towards each other
green algae	algae in the phylum Chlorophyta where the chlorophyll pigment is not masked by other pigments
Gulf of Maine	the coastal waters lying between the tip of Nova Scotia and Cape Cod
Gulf Stream	warm ocean current in the northern Atlantic Ocean, that flows out of the Gulf of Mexico
habitat	the place where a plant or animal lives
heat capacity	the amount of heat needed to raise the temperature of a body one degree
herbivore	plant-eating
hypothesis	an idea tentatively accepted to explain certain facts that with more substantial evidence is formulated into a theory
infrared	invisible light with wave lengths longer than those of visible light; thermal radiation
ingest	to eat
intercellular	among or between cells
interstitial	pertaining to space between one thing and another, like sand grains
intertidal	area between high- and low-tide marks
invagination	drawing into a sheath or covering
iridescent	having colors like the rainbow
isosceles	a triangle that has two equal sides
kelp	various large brown seaweeds
knot	one nautical mile per hour
liter	metric unit of volume; approximately the capacity of one quart
littoral region	zone between high- and low-tide marks
lunar	having to do with the moon
lunule	in bivalves, the heart-shaped impression on the outside of the shell, one-half of which is on each valve just below the top
macroscopic	visible to the naked eye
mantle	the fold of skin in mollusks that covers all or part of the body
medusoid	free-swimming, sexual form of coelenterates; jellyfish-like
membrane	a thin film or skin that covers part of an animal or plant or cell
meter	metric unit of distance; approximately 39.37 inches
microscopic	so small that it is invisible without the use of a microscope
mollusk	any animal of the phylum Mollusca characterized by a soft unsegmented body usually protected by a calcareous shell
motility	ability to move

multinucleate	having more than one nucleus
nacre	mother-of-pearl
neap tide	a tide of minimum range occurring at the first and third quarters of the moon
necton	the organisms swimming actively in water
nematocyst	a stinging cell located in the tentacles of coelenterates
neural	pertaining to nerves and the nervous system
nitrate	a salt formed from nitric acid that makes up the main source of nitrogen for most plants; $-NO_3$
nitrite	a form of nitrogen used by plants; $-NO_2$
nitrogen	N; a common non-metallic element that makes up 78 percent of the atmosphere as N_2; is an important constituent of proteins and nucleic acids
nitrogen-fixer	any of various organisms involved in the process of taking nitrogen from the atmosphere and using it to make protein or fixed forms of nitrogen
nodule	small knot-like structure on legume plants where nitrogen fixation takes place
notochord	a skeletal rod that lies lengthwise between the central nervous system and the gut. Occurs at some stage of development of all chordates
nucleus	a round mass without which most cells cannot live; contains the reproductive material and acts as the brain of the cell
ocular	of or pertaining to the eye
operculum	a horny plate attached to the foot of some gastropods which may act like a trap door, closing the aperture of the shell
osculum	a pore or opening in sponges
overturn	turn over; especially in reference to a body of water that is unstable and the bottom water rises to replace the surface water
palial sinus	a bend in the line that marks where the mantle is attached, on the interior of a shell of a bivalve
paleontologist	a scientist that studies fossils
papilla	a small nipple-like projection on an animal; pl. papillae
parapodium	the paired, segmentally arranged lateral projection of an annelid worms bearing bristles; pl. parapodia
parts per thousand	unit used for salinity; 1 part salt for every 1000 parts of water; o/ooo
periodicity	regular intervals in which an organism does certain things
periostracum	the layer of horny material covering the outer skin of shelled mollusks
pH	negative log of the hydrogen ion concentration; below seven is acid; seven is neutral; above seven is basic or alkaline
Phaeophyta	phylum of algae that has chlorophyll masked by brown pigments
phosphate	$-PO_4$; a salt or ester or organic compound of phosphoric acid
phosphorus	P; a nonmetallic element of the nitrogen family that occurs in combined form and is found in minerals, soils, water, bones and teeth

photic zone	the surface waters that are penetrated by sunlight, in which photosynthesis takes place
photosynthesis	a process used by organisms that contain chlorophyll, taking light and making carbohydrates from carbon dioxide and water
phycocyanin	pigment of the blue-green algae
phycoerythrin	pigment of the red algae
phylum	one of the primary divisions of the animal or plant kingdom; pl. phyla
phytoplankton	drifting plants
pigment	coloring matter in plants and animals; in plants the pigments are photosensitive
pigmentation	arrangement of coloring matter in an organ or organism
plankton	marine or freshwater plants and animals that drift with the movement of the water
plastid	a cell body that is not nucleus, usually containing pigments
pleopods	swimmerettes; paired appendages on the abdomen of crabs, lobsters and shrimp
pollution	a state of uncleanliness or impurity brought about by man's actions
pore	an opening
posterior	at or toward the tail end of the body
primary production	conversion of solar energy to chemical energy by the process of photosynthesis
proboscis	a muscular protrusible part of the digestive system
propagate	to multiply
protein	a substance found in most living matter, made of amino acids. Composed of oxygen, hydrogen, carbon, nitrogen and sometimes sulphur and phosphorus
protoplasm	living cell material
pseudofeces	excrement-like substance
pteropod	sea butterfly; a class of mollusks that have the lobes of their feet shaped like broad thin wings with which they swim
pulmonate	having lungs
radiolarians	organisms that have siliceous skeletons; usually microscopic
radula	a tongue-like organ of gastropods having teeth that may scrape, grind or bore; it tears up food and conveys it into the mouth
red algae	phylum Rhodophyta; red pigment masks the chlorophyll
red tide	seawater discolored by the presence of large numbers of dinoflagellates in amounts harmful to many forms of marine life
reflect	turn or fold back on itself; to throw back light
regenerate	to renew or grow again, like a crab growing a new claw
reproductive	capable of reproduction or formation of a new individual
respiration	the give and take of gas between an organism and its environment
respiratory	pertaining to breathing

rhizomes	an underground root-like stem that sends leafy shoots up and roots down
Rhodophyta	a phylum of marine algae in which red phycoerythrin and sometimes blue phycocyanin masks the chlorophyll
rostrum	a beak-like process above the mouth on a shell as on a lobster or shrimp shell
salinity	saltiness; concentration of salt
salt marsh	flat land that is daily submerged in salt water and has shore plants, usually grasses, growing on it
scatter	to reflect irregularly as from a piece of ground glass
scavenger	an animal that eats food killed or discarded by other animals
sea ice	ice formed by the freezing of sea water; does not retain seawater salinity levels
sea smoke	fog resulting at low temperatures when the water temperature exceeds the air temperature
seaweed	plants growing in the sea; algae
semi-diurnal	occurring twice daily
sessile	fastened to the bottom; non-moving
seta	the bristle or hair of invertebrates; pl. setae
sexual reproduction	reproduction of forming of new individuals by the joining of male and female gametes
sheath	a protective coating or covering
siliceous	containing silica or silicate
siphon	a tube for drawing or ejecting water
siphoneous	having a tube made of membrane that resembles or acts like a siphon
species	a category of plants or animals of distinctive characteristics that do and may interbreed and pass on these characteristics
spore	reproductive cell of plants; dormant form of certain plants
spring tide	a tide of greater than average range between high and low tide that occurs twice each month around the times of new and full moon when the tidal actions of the sun and moon are nearly in the same direction
starch	carbohydrate commonly formed by plants
stellate	star-shaped
stolon	root-like part of a colony of animals
stress	a physical, chemical, or emotional force to which an individual must make an adaptation or die
sublittoral	shallow-water zone to about 200 meters; below the littoral
submerge	to cover or overflow with water
substrate	substance upon which organisms can lodge and find housing
supralittoral	seashore above the high-water mark or spray area
surf	the swell of the sea that breaks upon the surface
swarmers	small organisms that can move, generally during plant reproduction

swimmerette	one of a pair of appendages on the abdomen of lobsters, crabs and shrimp
telson	the last segment of the abdomen of an arthropod
terrestrial	living on land
test	shell of an echinoid
theory	an idea that is based on substantial evidence.
thermocline	quite abrupt change in water temperature in relation to depth
thorax	the part of arthropods between the head and the abdomen
tide pool	a pool left usually in a rock basin by an ebbing tide
tides	the alternate rising and falling of the surface of the ocean that occurs twice a day and is caused by the gravitational attraction of the sun and moon, occurring unequally on different parts of the earth
tide table	a table that shows the height and time of the tide at specific locations during every 24-hour period throughout the year
torsion	the twisting undergone by gastropod mollusks in the larval stage
trade wind	a wind blowing almost constantly in the Northern Hemisphere from the northeast toward the equator
tubercules	small knob-like protuberances on plants or animals
ultraviolet	invisible light with wave lengths shorter than those of visible light
umbilicus	a central cavity at base of a snail shell where the whorls join
unicellular	composed of only one cell
valve	one part or one shell of a bivalve mollusk.
vascular	pertaining to vessels or tube which conduct fluid
vegetative	stage of growth in plants; non-reproductive
ventral	pertaining to the part of animal normally directed downwards by gravity, except in man whose ventral side is directed forward; the opposite of dorsal.
vertical current	current flowing up and down rather than back and forth
visceral	pertaining to the intestines
visible light	the radiation in a wave length that can be seen by the human eye
waning	to decrease in size or amount; to flow out or ebb
wave length	the distance from a certain point on one wave to that same point on the next wave
waves	moving ridges on the surface of the sea
waxing	to increase in size; to flow in or flood
westerlies	winds blowing from the west
whorl	one of the twists of a gastropod shell
xanthophylls	yellow or brown pigments found in the plastids
zooid	one individual of a colony of animals joined together
zooplankton	drifting animals
zoospore	a gamete that moves with a flagella; produced by asexual reproduction

Index of organisms
by common and scientific names

LIBRARY
SOUTHERN MAINE VOCATIONAL
TECHNICAL INSTITUTE

SOUTHERN MAINE TECHNICAL COLLEGE
The sea is all about us
QH 105 .M4 R62

3 6470 00005719 3

The Sea is all about us

Published by
The Peabody Museum
of Salem and
The Cape Ann Society for
Marine Science, Inc.

$6.25

Robbins, Director
body Museum of
Salem, and Clarice M. Yentsch, scientist at
the Bigelow Laboratory for Ocean Sciences,
McKown Point, West Boothbay Harbor, ME
04575, with drawings by Mary Ann Lash
and photographs by Mark Sexton.

*"For those who wish to familiarize them-
selves with the seashore populations and
the general ecology around Cape Ann and
other northern New England waters, for
text and illustrations this is the best hand-
book that I have yet seen for the serious
student or the enthusiastic amateur. It has
been a great help to me in my expeditions
in search of added knowledge and extra
enjoyment of Nature along this wonderful
stretch of the famed New England Coast."*

John Kieran

W7-AWJ-641